A Spanish Prisoner in the Ruins of Napoleon's Empire

A Spanish Prisoner in the Ruins of Napoleon's Empire

The Diary of
FERNANDO BLANCO WHITE'S
Flight to Freedom

Edited, with an Introduction, by
Christopher Schmidt-Nowara

Louisiana State University Press
Baton Rouge

Published by Louisiana State University Press

Manufactured in the United States of America
FIRST PRINTING

DESIGNER: *Mandy McDonald Scallan*
TYPEFACE: *Whitman*
PRINTER AND BINDER: *Sheridan Books*

The 1815 Diario of Fernando Blanco White is located in the Blanco White Family Collection (C0075), Manuscripts Division, Department of Rare Books and Special Collections, Princeton University Library, and is reproduced here with permission of Princeton University Library.

Library of Congress Cataloging-in-Publication Data are available from the Library of Congress.

ISBN 978-0-8071-6854-7 (cloth: alk. paper) — ISBN 978-0-8071-6855-4 (pdf) — ISBN 978-0-8071-6856-1 (epub)

The paper in this book meets the guidelines for permanence and durability of the Committee on Production Guidelines for Book Longevity of the Council on Library Resources. ♾

CONTENTS

ILLUSTRATIONS

PREFACE

Christopher Schmidt-Nowara died unexpectedly after a brief illness on June 27, 2015, at the tragically young age of forty-eight. He had almost completed his last book, an edition of a journal by the Spanish lieutenant Fernando Blanco White (1786–1849), recounting Blanco White's flight to England in 1814 after five years of captivity in France. The diary was written in English; Professor Schmidt-Nowara produced an annotated transcription of the text and wrote an introduction. At the time of his death, the book had already been accepted by Louisiana State University Press and Professor Schmidt-Nowara was in the process of revision, expecting to submit the final manuscript to the press at the end of the summer.

The Schmidt-Nowara family deeded Christopher Schmidt-Nowara's scholarly papers, books, and intellectual property rights to Tufts University, where he held the Prince of Asturias Chair in Spanish Civilization in the Department of History. Both the family and LSU Press were enthusiastic about publishing the manuscript of the journal, and for this reason we decided to see it through to completion. Two of us have worked on this project: Beatrice F. Manz, chair of the Department of History, and Matthew Ehrlich, who was Professor Schmidt-Nowara's graduate student at the time of his death. In consultation with LSU Press, we decided to keep the manuscript as much as possible as we found it.

Among the papers that came to us, we found a revised version of the introduction, with a few notes for additional corrections and missing citations. The corrections were incorporated and the needed citations added; thus the introduction is probably very much as Professor Schmidt-Nowara would have published it. We found a list of illustrations planned for the edition and were able to identify and obtain most of these. Several maps were also planned but only one—the itinerary of Blanco White's journey—could be completed with the information available to us. At the suggestion of the outside reader for the press, Professor Schmidt-Nowara had intended to include translations of a few letters by Blanco White, but he had not begun work on them, and we therefore left them out. For the text of the diary, he had done some minor editing already, and the press's reader had suggested further light editing, since English was not Blanco White's native language. Professor Schmidt-Nowara and the press had agreed that there should be no attempt to render the diary into the English of a native speaker but that some changes should be made where the phrasing or vocabulary made the text difficult to understand. In the manuscript, only about 15 of the total 119 diary pages had been marked for corrections. We decided that instead of trying to guess what Professor Schmidt-Nowara would have done, we should simply leave the text as it was, changing the wording only where necessary for comprehension, and correcting obvious typographical errors and omissions, some punctuation, and one or two translations from French quotations. The papers in our possession do not include a facsimile of the original diary, so we have not attempted any comparisons of the transcription with the original. The reader should therefore understand that the diary text has been published without the final editing and checking that Professor Schmidt-Nowara would have provided.

We wish to acknowledge our debt to the many people who have helped with this project. First of all, we must thank Christopher Schmidt-Nowara's family, most particularly his sister and executor, Molly Schmidt-Nowara, for their generous gift and their help in locating papers and digital files relating to this project. Two editors at LSU Press have been enormously helpful: Alisa Plant, whose enthusiasm for the project encouraged us to take it on, and Rand Dotson, who has provided invaluable help and guidance throughout, from navigating the first legal issues to designing the final presentation of the manuscript. We thank the staff of the Rare Books and Special Collections Division of the Firestone Library, Princeton University, for permission to publish the text of the diary and to reproduce documents in the Blanco White Family Collection. Daniel Santamaria of the Tufts Archives was instrumental in arranging for the gift and working out the legal and financial issues of publication. Patrick Florance, of the Tisch Library at Tufts, has generously drawn the itinerary map for us free of charge. We also thank Joselyn Almeida-Beveridge for her help in launching the project and for educating us in the history of the Blanco White family. The staff of the Tufts Department of History, Annette Lazzara and Lori Piracini, have been endlessly helpful with paperwork and logistics, and the department itself has provided funds as needed.

Our colleagues at Tufts, Ina Baghdiantz-McCabe and Elizabeth Foster, have provided help, particularly with French translations and citations. Professor Schmidt-Nowara's outside colleagues have also been generous with their time; James Amelang supplied the references needed to complete the footnotes to the introduction, with the further assistance of Martin Murphy. The generous help of these people has made the publication of this book possible.

Beatrice Forbes Manz
Matthew Ehrlich

NOTE ON EDITORIAL METHOD

Fernando Blanco White was not a native English speaker, which presents two issues in transcribing the manuscript, especially the sections that are clearly in his hand. (It is likely that Louisa Moore and Joseph Blanco White occasionally served as amanuensis.) First, there are several awkward passages, and second, there are some corrections on the manuscript made by Fernando himself or by Joseph and Louisa. Regarding the first issue, I have decided to let the original version shine through as much as possible in order to give the reader a sense of his style, which, even if ungrammatical at times, was always lively, direct, and comprehensible. Regarding the second issue, many of the corrections are minor changes to prepositions, articles, or verb tenses. I felt that those sorts of corrections were not worth flagging in the edition because they did not change the meaning, and to signal each and every one would make reading the text tedious. Therefore, I have indicated only substantial editorial interventions, as well as the few marginal comments. I have also translated the occasional sentence or phrase in French or another language.

Christopher Schmidt-Nowara

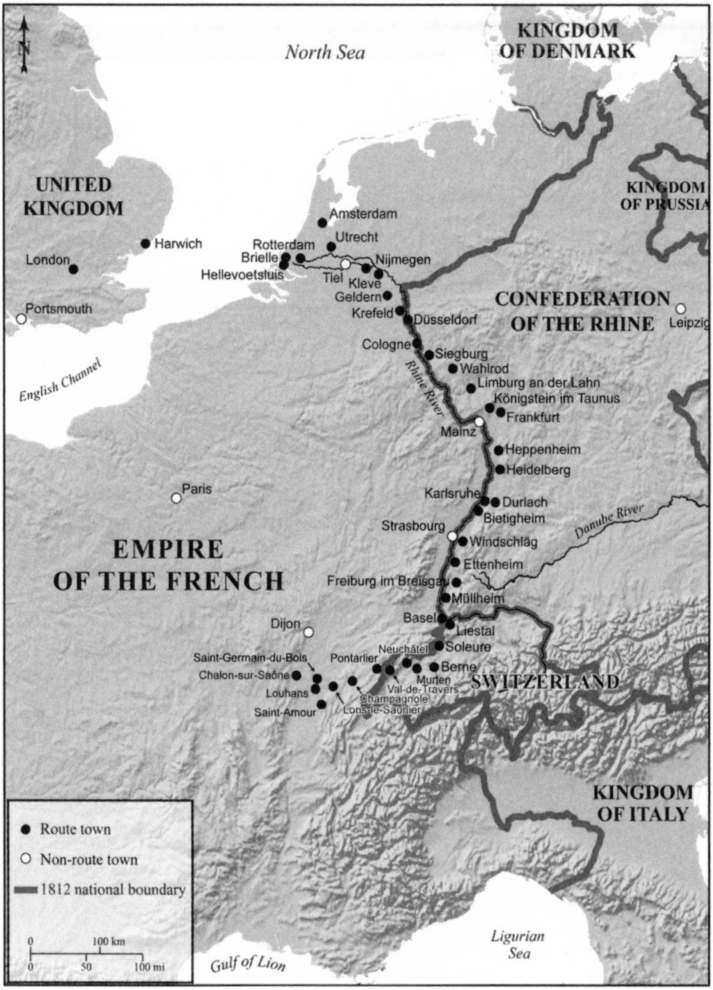

Fernando Blanco White's route

FERNANDO BLANCO WHITE'S ITINERARY
January–March 1814

January 6	Hopes to depart from Chalon-sur-Saône but must wait for the following day.
January 7	Departs with guide and nine other Spaniards, including the Porres brothers.
January 8	Spaniards reach Austrian forces at Saint-Germain-du-Bois, having spent the day hiding at a farmer's home in La Malporte, an adjacent hamlet.
January 9	Spaniards leave by cart in the afternoon for Louhans. Arrive late at night and are met by a mob, as the Austrians have not occupied the town. Forced from Louhans in the wee hours.
January 10	Spaniards arrive back in Austrian-held Saint-Germain early in the day. Depart again under Austrian protection. Reach Lons-le-Saunier at night.
January 11	Go to Saint-Amour in search of the Austrian commander.
January 12	Return to Lons-le-Saunier with passport entitling the party to transport, lodging, food.
January 13	Spaniards head into the Jura Mountains and Champagnole.
January 14–15	Proceed to Pontarlier, along the way meeting and incorporating Spanish soldiers working as peasants. In the environs of the fortress of Joux, which has fallen to the Austrians, commander grants Fernando and his party a layover day.
January 16	To Val-de-Travers, Switzerland, part of the way by sled.
January 17	To Neuchâtel.
January 18	To Murten by boat and on foot.
January 19	To Bern by cart.
January 20	To Soleure by cart.

January 21	To Liestal by cart, after being rebuffed in Waldenburg.
January 22–23	To Basel by cart. Encounter José Pizarro, Spanish minister to the king of Prussia.
January 24	Walk to Mülheim.
January 25	To Freiburg on foot and by cart. Manuel Porres falls ill. Fernando and the Porres brothers remain as he convalesces, supported by French émigrés.
February 21	Spaniards depart Freiburg in style, having purchased a charabanc and horses, and hired a servant. Rest in Ettenheim after being rebuffed in Kenzingen.
February 22	Rebuffed at Offenburg and told to lodge in Windschläg, close to Strasbourg.
February 23	To Bietigheim, after being rebuffed at Rastatt and then lost on the road.
February 24	To Durlach, after stop in Karlsruhe.
February 25	To Heidelberg.
February 26	Make a short trip to Heppenheim.
February 27–28	To Frankfurt, where the Austrian commander gives them permission to stay more than one night.
March 1	To Königstein.
March 2	To Limburg, where they see troops setting off for the siege of Mainz.
March 3	To Wahlrod. Rudely received in several villages.
March 4	To Siegburg.
March 5	To Cologne.
March 6	Backtrack to Düsseldorf.
March 7	Have trouble crossing the ice-bound Rhine en route to Krefeld.
March 8	To Geldern on bitterly cold, snowy day.
March 9–10	To Nijmegen in Holland, via Kleve. Poorly received.
March 11	Head across the dykes to Utrecht via Tiel, where they disembark from their carriage for the last time and continue by cart.
March 12–13	To Amsterdam. Fernando attempts to find his bankers, with some luck.
March 14	To Rotterdam by diligence.

March 15	In Rotterdam, meet Spanish consul. Head toward Hellevoetsluis, where an Englishman, Captain King, is charged with evacuating Spanish refugees. Marooned at night on island across from Brielle.
March 16	Cross over to Brielle by boat in the morning. Find many other Spaniards congregated. Fernando and party are housed here while they wait for a ship.
March 17	Fernando walks to Hellevoetsluis with Mr. Manuel to check on Captain King and the possibility of sailing to England.
March 18	Decides to return to Hellevoetsluis the next day and pay for passage instead of waiting uncertainly for a free passage from Brielle.
March 19	Spaniards purchase passage at great expense (£ 2.14.6 each). But not for "our poor Estevan," whom the party leaves in Brielle.
March 20	To Hellevoetsluis, but the weather is so bad that Captain King delays departure until the next day.
March 21	Set sail with a crowded ship and cosmopolitan group. Uncomfortable night aboard.
March 22	Arrive in Harwich. Cold reception improves when Fernando receives letter informing him that as a Briton he needs no permission from the ambassador to travel to London. Departs that evening by coach with fat Dutchman. Porres brothers remain in Harwich.
March 23	Arrives in London around noon after a difficult journey by coach. Disembarks in Cheapside with the Dutchman, who finds Fernando a hackney coach that takes him to Joseph's home in 67 Edgware Road.

A Spanish Prisoner
in the Ruins of
Napoleon's Empire

Introduction

Spain's war of independence against France between 1808 and 1814 opened a protracted political crisis that transformed not only peninsular Spain but also the vast overseas empire in the Americas. For the next three decades, Spaniards would fight in wars of resistance, civil wars, and colonial counterinsurgencies as they struggled to rid their country of foreign occupiers, fought among themselves over their country's form of government, and sought to maintain control over the colonial empire. During these long years of conflict, thousands of Spanish soldiers and civilians were driven from their homes. Some were internal refugees fleeing war and invasions; others were exiles forced abroad by political changes. Many were prisoners of war who languished in camps and jails far from their homeland.

The diary of Lt. Fernando Blanco White (1786–1849), in which he recounts his flight to freedom in 1814 after five years of captivity in France, introduces us to the experiences of displacement, imprisonment, and expatriation that were so prevalent in Spain's revolutionary

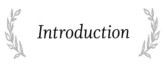

James Amelang, Rafe Blaufarb, Claudia Guarisco, Martin Murphy, Alisa Plant, and an anonymous referee read drafts of this introduction. My thanks to them for their many questions and insights. Thanks also to Angel Loureiro for an invitation to present a version of the introduction to the Department of Spanish and Portuguese at Princeton, where I benefited greatly from his comments and those of Arcadio Diaz-Quiñones, Germán Labrador Méndez, and Stanley Stein. Special thanks to Jeremy Adelman and Martin Murphy for their encouragement from the beginning of this research.—CSN era. In the context of Spain's War of Independence, his diary offers rich insights into the plight of the tens of thousands of Spaniards who found themselves in a similar situation at the end of the struggle against the Napoleonic Empire. They were far from home, cut off from their families, apparently abandoned—if not actively persecuted—by their government, and utterly uncertain of how and when they might return to Spain. The diary also provides an engrossing picture of Europe in this moment of profound flux and confusion, as the order constructed by Napoleon came tumbling down and the monarchical powers of Britain and Central and Eastern Europe marched through France to restore the old regime. Fernando's many encounters, quarrels, and conversations during his two-month sojourn usher the reader into the quotidian aspects of this exceptional, uncertain moment in the heart of Europe and, implicitly, in Fernando's own distant and elusive homeland, Spain.

THE BLANCO WHITES

The diary, along with Fernando's letters and numerous other papers, is held in Princeton's Firestone Library in the Blanco White Family Collection. The distinguished scholar of Spanish history and literature Vicente Llorens brought the collection to Princeton, largely because of his interest in the life and work of Fernando's famous—infamous to some—brother Joseph. Llorens was the author of a study of the Spanish exiles in England in the 1820s and 1830s. The most brilliant of these exiles at that time was Joseph, who had arrived in London in 1810 and would never again return to his native land.[1] Scholars have consulted the ample collection at Princeton chiefly to write about Joseph, a striking figure during the Hispanic world's revolutionary epoch and a prolific autobiographer.[2] His most lasting accomplishment was the newspaper *El Español*, which he almost single-handedly wrote, edited, and produced between 1810 and 1814 during his early London exile. *El Español* includes some of the most acute commentary on politics in Spain and Spanish America during this period. It was likely the most widely read publication in Spanish at the time because of the sponsorship and distribution carried out by the British Foreign Office.[3] Joseph has also attracted widespread interest because he served as an important bridge between Spanish and British literature, playing a key role in confirming generally negative English views of Spain and the Catholic Church, most famously through his *Letters from Spain* (1822).[4] His religious preoccupations and conversions have also fascinated scholars. In Spain, he had been a Catholic priest, though a highly skeptical one who fathered a son (Ferdinand White, who would later join him in England and be raised as a Briton). In exile, he converted to Anglicanism and became a minister of the Church of England. Yet late in life, he abandoned the Church of England, leaving behind many friends and powerful patrons, to live in some seclusion and misery as a Unitarian. He died in Liverpool in 1841.[5]

In writing his diary, Fernando followed his brother by choosing the name Blanco White, rather than using their original Spanish surnames, Blanco y Crespo. On their father's side, the Blancos were descended from Irish merchants, the Whites, who immigrated to Seville in the early eighteenth century "to escape the oppression of the penal laws."[6] Their grandfather's business flourished in Seville, and the family was rewarded by the Spanish monarchy: "They lived in the best style then known in that part of Spain. The king of Spain granted to our family all the privileges of the Spanish *Noblesse*, in perpetuity."[7] Their father, Guillermo, who was widely traveled but apparently not an astute businessman, changed the family name to Blanco and married into the local gentry; Joseph (originally José María Blanco y Crespo) adopted both names when he arrived in London in 1810.

Though thoroughly integrated into Andalusian and Spanish society, the Blancos nonetheless retained important links to Britain and Ireland through the family business as merchants and through their community of Irish migrants to Seville, including cousins with whom they shared their business, the Cahills and the Becks. They formed "a small Irish colony, whose members preserve the language and many of the habits and affections which its founders brought to Spain."[8] Those connections would serve both brothers well. Joseph could join the London and Oxford milieu, though he never felt completely at peace, while Fernando, when he crossed the English Channel from Holland, found his passage to London greatly eased because he was considered a Briton. Presumably, the brothers had the rudiments of English from a young age. Joseph certainly became an accomplished author in that language, and Fernando wrote his diary in English, though it shows evidence of some editing, most likely by Joseph and the family friend Louisa Moore. After Fernando returned to Seville in 1816, his correspondence with Joseph was sometimes in English.

Joseph's life was defined by his rejection of Spain and by his religious inquietude, themes elaborated at length in his autobiographical writings. At the time that Fernando wrote his diary, he too yearned to remain in England, perhaps for good. In several letters to his parents, he outlined a plan to study English intensively and to take a position in the merchant house of Gordon and Murphy, where he could learn more about trade with Europe and the Americas.[9] Spain, in contrast, was a dead end; all he could expect was a resumption of military duties, which no longer interested him. Even worse, if he were sent to the American colonies, a return to the army would undoubtedly prove fatal.[10] Though none of his letters or his diary demonstrate the constant religious preoccupations that framed Joseph's public and private writings, Fernando seems to have shared some of his brother's contempt for the Catholic clergy, and he peppered his diary with anticlerical comments as he traveled through the Catholic Rhineland. For example, he dismissed Cologne "as a priest-ridden town," the proof of which was not only the plethora of church steeples he viewed as he approached the city but also the relative poverty of the surrounding landscape, a sure sign in his estimation of the Church's dead hand: "I was confirmed in my opinion when I saw the sterility and unpopulousness of the country."

But while there were inklings that Fernando hoped to follow, at least in part, in his brother's footsteps, he eventually had to return to a much more conventional life. When their father Guillermo died in 1816, it was Fernando who journeyed to Seville to take care of the family's interests. He was "purified" by the military inspectors, even though his many years in France and his desire to stay in England would have made him suspect, as would his membership in the Freemasons, which he joined while in the French depots—though that apparently remained secret.[11] He married his cousin Juana María Olloqui y Estrada, continued his military service, and took part in the intellectual, educational, and commercial life of Seville for the next three decades as the Belgian consul and as an instructor in English at the University of Seville, the Escuela Normal Militar de Enseñanza Mutua, and the Escuelas Lancasterianas de Niñas. He also held positions in Seville's municipal government, a burden about which he complained to his brother in several letters.[12]

Though he was a prominent figure in the city's cultural life, Fernando had less success in business—a legacy, it would seem, of his father's poor management. His cousin Lucas Beck was now the primary figure in the family business, and Fernando remained unsure of his stake and his claims. This uncertainty also made Joseph's life in Britain economically precarious because he relied on remittances from his brother, in addition to the monies he earned as a writer and tutor. Such family support was especially important to Joseph when it came time to educate his son Ferdinand and to start him in a military career. Financial issues would remain a constant theme in the correspondence between the two brothers, though Fernando succeeded in some measure in sheltering Joseph from the unpleasant truth of their situation. An 1819 letter from Fernando to Joseph captures both the vitality of the family connection and the constant preoccupation with their uncertain fortunes.

> I shall do everything in my power to set your mind at ease about my welfare; but as for admitting of your more than generous cession of all your property in Spain you must see that I could never do it while you are living, not even after your death

AVE Y MARÍA.

Recibí de Dn Fernando Blanco treinta y cinco rs de vellon limosna de siete Misas rezad. que por el alma de su Hermano Dn Jose maria Blanco Difunto mandó aplicar en el Altar de las sagradas Cárceles de las SS. VV, y MM. Justa y Rufina, en el cual por Bula del Sr. Gregorio XIII dada en 15 de Agosto de 1583 se goza de una Indulgencia para que el alma por quien se aplicare, mediante los méritos de Ntro. Sr. Jesucristo, de la Bienaventurada Virgen Maria y de los Bienaventurados Apóstoles S. Pedro y S. Pablo, y todos los demas Santos, sea libre de las penas del Purgatorio, con la condicion precisa de ser la Misa celebrada por Sacerdote Trinitario y Conventual de esta Casa. Y por ser verdad doy el presente en este Real Monasterio de Sta. Justa y Rufina, del celestial y primitivo Orden de la Sma. Trinidad Redencion de Cautivos, extramuros de Sevilla, en 3 del mes de Enero del año de 1842

Son 7 Misas rezadas
Limosna 35 rs. vn.

Fr Juan Jose Mantez
Colector

Receipt of payment by Fernando Blanco White for masses for his brother Joseph Blanco White, who died in 1841. (Blanco White Family Collection [C0075], Manuscripts Division, Department of Rare Books and Special Collections, Princeton University Library)

(if I am to see that) for the sake of little F.o [Ferdinand]. Your cession might put your mind at ease, but it would undoubtedly put mine in the wrack. I know that my remittances can never be considerable enough to be worth your while, but you can accumulate them . . . and this little stock may be very useful to you for some emergency. I am too cautious, am I not? But you are a little careless in money matters.[13]

Unlike his brother, Fernando seems to have made peace with the predominance of the Catholic Church once he had settled back into his Seville life. One of his sons was to enter the priesthood, much to the dismay of Ferdinand, who wrote to his uncle: "I cannot help wishing you had made my cousin a soldier instead of a parson but of course you know best on this subject."[14] When Joseph died in 1841, Fernando paid for masses to be said for him in Seville, which likely would have surprised and perhaps displeased Joseph himself.[15] Joseph's posthumously published *Life* spoke of his living in Spain as a priest as "mental slavery," a phrase that he evoked repeatedly in his British writings on Spain and the Catholic Church.[16] He might have surmised that his beloved younger brother suffered under the same yoke after his return to Seville.

THE WAR OF INDEPENDENCE

At the time of the French invasion and attempted conquest of the Iberian Peninsula in 1808, the mood in the enlightened and patriotic circles of Seville was one not of servitude but of liberation. Spain and France had been unequal allies since the mid-1790s, when, according to the terms of the Treaty of Basel (1795), Spain was to provide France with monies, supplies, and troops in its protracted wars against its many European foes. French troops were also garrisoned on Spanish soil, but the alliance was obviously an uneasy one. Though the two monarchies had forged effective alliances over the course of the eighteenth century (the Family Compacts between the two Bourbon dynasties), the French Revolution, the execution of Louis XVI, and the declaration of the Republic had placed them on opposite ends of the political and ideological spectrum.

This unusual and asymmetrical partnership tipped even further in France's favor with the ascent of Napoleon. His ambition to exclude British trade from the European continent put the Iberian Peninsula squarely in his crosshairs. Portugal, Britain's closest European ally and protégé, was a tempting target for both France and Spain; France could shut Britain out of the Iberian Peninsula, while Spain hoped for territorial gains in its neighboring kingdom. The French invasion, facilitated by the Spanish government, led to the evacuation of the Portuguese Court to Rio de Janeiro in 1808, under British protection. It also opened the door to Napoleon for more ruthless dealings with the Spanish Bourbons, whose intrigues and infighting had made him despair of them as effective allies. To that end, while his troops occupied the capital city, Madrid, he enticed Charles IV and his son Ferdinand VII, who had suddenly displaced his father as king of Spain through a palace putsch, to the French city of Bayonne. Though the stated purpose of the invitation was to reconcile father and son, the real goal was to place the court under his power and to give the throne to his brother, Joseph Bonaparte, Joseph I of Spain.[17]

News of these machinations touched off a rebellion in Madrid, the famous 2nd of May rising. The French forces quickly and brutally suppressed the insurgency, but they nonetheless were insecure in the capital because Spanish armies gained unexpected victories in the field, most notably at Bailén in Andalusia. Joseph I and his court departed the capital in the summer but returned to recapture Madrid later in the year, with Napoleon and his crack troops at the fore.[18]

Fernando's native Andalusia was a site of resistance to the French occupation. The battle of Bailén in mid-July was a major victory that halted the French advance into the region and led Joseph Bonaparte to evacuate Madrid shortly thereafter. On the political side, the Junta of Seville, one of the many local governing bodies of resistance that sprang up in Spanish and Spanish American cities in 1808, sought to dominate the Central Junta, which had aimed, with only partial success, to unite all other patriotic juntas in the peninsula and in the overseas colonies. Until it fell to the French armies in 1810, Seville remained a vital center of Spanish defiance.[19]

Fernando joined the Third Volunteers of Seville on June 28, 1808, as a junior officer and marched north to defend Madrid against Napoleon's approaching armies. His letter home to his father on November 29 was, in hindsight, ominous, as he discussed his destination and expected engagement with the French: "Today at 10 in the morning we are marching toward Somosierra where they say the Battalion is."[20] That would be the last news that the family had directly from Fernando until February of the following year. Somosierra, in the mountains north of Madrid, was where the French routed the Spanish

Bataille du Col de Sonio-Sierra (Castille) le 30 novembre 1808, by Louis-François Lejeune. The French routed the Spanish during the Battle of Somosierra, and Fernando Blanco White was captured only a few days later. (Erich Lessing/Art Resource, NY)

Napoleon Accepting the Capitulation of Madrid, December 4, 1808, by Antoine-Jean Gros (1771–1836). (© RMN-Grand Palais/Art Resource, NY)

defenders on November 30, sending them into retreat. A few days later, French armies once again occupied Madrid, and this time they would remain. The broken Spanish armies retreated beyond the Tagus River, and thousands of civilians also fled the city. But many Spaniards remained behind and would soon find themselves marching in the opposite direction. Like thousands of other soldiers and officers, Fernando fell captive to the invaders on December 4, the day of Madrid's surrender to Napoleon, and was deported from his home country to a distant depot of prisoners in eastern France. He was sent first to Dijon, then to Chalon-sur-Saône, where he spent the majority of the war until his flight in January 1814.

A brief letter dated February 1809 told his parents of his arrival in France. While Fernando sought to soothe them, he also made clear his want and insecurity.

> Tomorrow I leave for Dijon, which is my destination. You can send me some aid there because I am in need of it. Nonetheless, I endure the labors of a prisoner with health and happiness. You above all my Mother should convince yourself that the labors I am undergoing do not exceed my strength and therefore should not cause you an unfruitful feeling that could make you lose your health and even your life. . . . Although I am in great want I have not lacked for those who have helped me with some shoes, some boots, with a hat etc.[21]

A year later, when he found himself in a more secure situation, he wrote at length about his capture in Madrid and the hardships that he suffered on the road to his imprisonment in France.

> I was made prisoner on the 4th of December of 808 [*sic*] in Madrid where I remained until the 15th; shut up in the casa de la China, from which I left with 8 *duros* for a journey of 350 leagues on the 17th. Because I didn't have any money I decided not to bring my horse or my bag because I feared that I would

> die of hunger. The travails on the road were imponderable. They gave us bread and meat, when there was some, and we cooked it with water and some times with salt. We walked on foot and almost unshod seven leagues every day. When we had a long day of walking they would not let us rest so we had to eat a piece of black bread, like *pan de munición*, while we were walking. The cold was insufferable, as strong as it is here, and the ice so hard that we fell with every step. Sleeping on the ground was now the custom, and the lice were in our cloths. The closer we came to Bayonne, our luck improved in terms of lodgings, and once we entered France they gave us ten *reales* every day to support ourselves. They lodged us in inns so we had beds but we had to sleep two in each of them, which disgusted me infinitely.[22]

The imprisonment that he suffered was less brutal than other experiences of captivity in Europe and the Americas during the revolutionary era, but it had its conflicts and share of hardships, which Fernando described in detail in his letters.[23] French government reports show that there were frequent attempts at escape.[24] The reprisals could be serious. Fernando noted that his friend Juan María Maestre had tried to flee but was caught and locked away in the fortress of Joux, "penniless."[25] Such a terrible fate was always in the offing during his captivity. In 1810 he explained, "Because the prisoners in the depots are constantly escaping they are treating us more rigorously than before. We have roll call three times a day and they will not give us passes to visit friends in other depots. Anyone without a list justifying his conduct is punished with 8 days of arrest. Anyone caught in the act of escaping is punished with one month in the dungeon and prison at the discretion of the Minister, which is to say, confinement until the end of the war."[26]

He also described the wretched conditions under which he lived for practically the first year of his captivity until monies from his family finally arrived and allowed him some temporary comfort and security. When he arrived in Dijon on February 16, 1809, after a two-month journey from Madrid, he was housed in the barracks with other Spanish prisoners, men and officers alike. The modest salary paid out by the French, a percentage of his officer's pay, forced him and his companions to cook for themselves, even though none of them knew how to do so. The food was necessarily bad under such conditions, though after several days he had learned how to cook like "the best Spanish chef." However, the living conditions could not be improved in the barracks; the men were "infested by lice," and given the continuous state of noise and disruption, Fernando thought that "living in a brothel would be better." He was finally able to borrow some money from a friend and received permission to live in a rented room outside the barracks in Autun, where they had been moved in July. Having to pay rent meant that he could afford to prepare only one meal a day, thus suffering "continuous hunger that ceaselessly tormented me." Finally, at the end of December 1809, the "guardian angel brought me the help that you had sent," and, now back in Dijon, he could afford to provide for himself.[27]

The relative stability of his existence in Dijon was disrupted when he and other Spaniards were moved to Chalon-sur-Saône in October 1811. Once again, his letters show concern about the transfer of monies from Seville and the difficulties of receiving correspondence from his parents. The agent in Bayonne charged with the transfers was unreliable, and Fernando frequently complained that he might go weeks at a time without news from Seville, blaming it on lost mail. Loans from Spanish friends, to be repaid when they were freed or by his parents back home, held him over until the monthly disbursements once again flowed.[28] They did so in 1812, apparently thanks to the intervention of his brother Joseph, yet Fernando's letters from the last months of his captivity in Chalon are cryptic (undoubtedly to evade censorship) and bitter. He spoke of his "slavery" in January 1813 and, in letters dated from the summer and fall, mentioned without elaboration the increasing "humiliations" of his situation, even as he assured his parents that he remained healthy and active, playing music

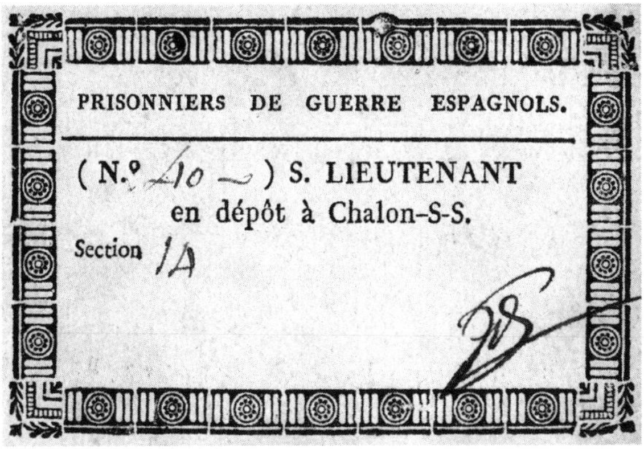
PRISONNIERS DE GUERRE ESPAGNOLS.

(N.° 10) S. LIEUTENANT
en dépôt à Chalon-S-S.
Section 1A

Prison pass, Chalon-sur-Saône. (Blanco White Family Collection [C0075]; Manuscripts Division, Department of Rare Books and Special Collections, Princeton University Library)

(a theme in the account of his escape across Europe) and studying mathematics.[29] Long gone were the days in Dijon when he had applied to his parents for money to spend a month in Paris, Europe's capital of arts and sciences, if he could negotiate a pass: "It would be painful if I returned to Spain without having seen Paris, having been almost at its gates."[30] In the end, he did not travel to Paris, but he did see dozens of French, Swiss, German, and Dutch villages, towns, and cities during his trek through Europe in the winter of 1814.

Fernando, then, began his captivity in France in desperate conditions, forced to march with a defeated army from Madrid to Dijon in the winter of 1808–9. He endured a hard year, living largely in the barracks, experiencing hunger when he tried to live outside them, out of touch with his family, and without crucial financial support from them. By the end of 1809 and for almost the next two years, his situation seems to have been secure; funds were forthcoming, and there was almost an ebullience to some of his letters, as when he spoke of his plan to pass a month in Paris. He called Dijon "a second homeland."[31] One might speculate that it was the great triumph of French arms in Spain—the conquest of Andalusia in 1810 and the domination of virtually the entire country for a brief time—that gave some stability to his distant connection with his parents in Seville, the necessary lifeline. That mood came to an end quickly in the fall of 1811, when he and other Spaniards moved to Chalon-sur-Saône. Being uprooted left him to start anew, "like the first day when I arrived in France."[32] Though some of the correspondence from Chalon-sur-Saône is upbeat, for the most part it details his financial uncertainty, brought about by the tenuousness of his connection with Seville. He was on sounder footing in 1812, but his mood was clearly restless and embittered, no doubt exacerbated by the trauma of the Napoleonic regime as it hurled itself unsuccessfully against Russia and experienced major setbacks in Spain at the hands of the guerrillas and the Duke of Wellington's Anglo-Portuguese army. Indeed, in that year, the emperor ordered that the pay issued to prisoners be reduced. Resources were going elsewhere, and those changes affected Fernando's daily life.[33] The breakdown of the first Empire at the end of 1813 and the beginning of 1814 was welcome to him, as he now could conceivably flee to freedom without too much fear of recapture and reprisal, though anxiety about that, as the diary attests, was never absent.

FLIGHT

Fernando's insecurity and desperation during his flight were captured by various official accounts of the thousands of Spanish fugitives trekking across Western Europe. For example, writing from Basel on January 16, 1814, Spain's minister to the Prussian court communicated to Madrid the dire situation of the many Spaniards he encountered there. José Pizarro, a distinguished servant of the Spanish state throughout the various changes of government in the early nineteenth century, was in Basel instead of Berlin because he was following the Prussian king as he, his forces, and their Austrian and Russian allies rolled back the Napoleonic armies and pursued them into France. Pizarro's travels would soon find him in Paris with the victorious allies. Along the way, he recounted scenes like that in Basel: destitute Spaniards applying to him for funds to feed and clothe themselves and to make their way home to Spain. Most were escaped prisoners of war, like Fernando, but there were other categories of expatriates, as Pizarro later observed, including Spaniards who had fought with the Russians against Napoleon (the Alexander Regiment) and "los Jurados." The latter were collaborating Spaniards who swore an oath of loyalty to Joseph I, Napoleon's brother and proxy as king of Spain between 1808 and his retreat from the peninsula in 1813. This group, known to history as the *afrancesados,* would soon run afoul of the restored Spanish Bourbon monarch, Ferdinand VII, who would brand them as traitors and prohibit them from returning to Spain by a decree issued on May 30, 1814, just a few months after Pizarro's encounters with them.[34]

But the majority of those who sought Pizarro's assistance were Napoleon's Spanish prisoners, of whom there were some sixty thousand on French soil by the end of 1813.[35] Pizarro described their desperate situation in his dispatch from Basel, noting that as the Prussian and allied forces advanced, more and more Spaniards applied to him because

> these loyal soldiers have had more opportunity to escape. They present themselves to me practically naked and in need. They all demand aid but I am forced to deny it to them because, as Your Excellency knows, I have no authorization, and the latest order that I received from Your Excellency on the 31st of October prohibits me from making charges to my accounts without an accompanying order. My heart suffers unspeakably. Their replies and answers, often marked with the stamp of impatience and necessity, increase the difficulty of my position. I cannot persuade them that I have no powers and that I am genuinely lacking in means myself. I do not even have credit because of the uncertainty of where my journey will take me.

Finally, Pizarro reported that he could offer some assistance to the escapees in Basel because the British diplomat, Lord Aberdeen, gave him twenty gold Louis for that purpose.[36] The British would offer more assistance later, with Pizarro communicating that Lord Castlereagh, the foreign minister, had provided two hundred gold Louis in Châtillon-sur-Seine on February 10.[37] Only in the summertime would Pizarro receive funds from his own government to help the thousands of Spanish expatriates at large in Europe. On June 28, he acknowledged the authorization to draw money from the bank of DeRoure, by which time Napoleon's armies were defeated and Pizarro was taking part in the occupation of Paris. The restored absolutist regime of Ferdinand VII had since made it clear that not all Spaniards would be welcomed back and that even those who did return would have to undergo a process of "purification" to verify that they had neither betrayed their country nor fallen prey to revolutionary ideals. In other words, the restored monarch could be less than compassionate when it came to the plight of the thousands who had fought for his cause.[38]

Fernando was one of the Spaniards whom Pizarro met during that brief stay in Basel. Fernando's flight to freedom took him and a group of Spanish officers and soldiers through eastern France, Switzerland, the Rhineland, and the Netherlands and, finally, to England. (The core of this group were friends from his native Seville—the brothers José, Manuel, and Pedro Porres, sons of the Marquis of Castilleja—and their servant Estebán.) Their route was indirect because the fugitives had to travel through liberated European territories under the control of the allies. France itself was still a theater of war as Wellington's army pushed through the Pyrenees and southern France, the most direct route back to Spain and one that Fernando and thousands of other Spanish prisoners had traveled (in the opposite direction) several years earlier when they were captured. Meanwhile, Napoleon fought one last brilliant campaign in France's northern tier as he tried, futilely, to check the Prussians, Austrians, and Russians.[39]

Compared to thousands of his compatriots who followed the same road, Fernando was in an unusual situation because England was an advantageous destination for him. In general, the Spanish escapees and deserters who arrived in England from Holland were quickly moved to Portsmouth and then repatriated to the northern Spanish port city of San Sebastián. During their transit, they lived in miserable conditions because their government's representatives were themselves practically destitute and were powerless to aid the surge of refugees through Holland and England between December 1813 and the early summer months of 1814. The secretary of the Spanish embassy in London reported that, "I am under siege without being able to go out because the Ambassador's house is continuously surrounded by unfortunate Spaniards demanding help that I cannot provide. They will not leave until hunger forces them to beg scandalously and indecorously for alms."[40]

Fernando, because of his Irish parentage and his family connections in England, was spared such days of doubt and suffering once he arrived. As he recounts in the diary, he was whisked away from the port city of Harwich and reunited with Joseph in London. Fernando remained in England for two years, during which he composed this diary in English (the cover page dates it to 1815) with the assistance of others, most likely his brother and the family friend Louisa Moore. When he returned to Spain in 1816 to take over the family's affairs after the death of his father, he left the unpublished diary and other papers and books behind with Louisa's family. Though his brother sent it to him in Seville several years later, Fernando never published it. I speculate below about why he kept such a lively and insightful work in the desk drawer for so many years.[41] Had he published it, he would have given readers one of the few Spanish military memoirs of the period, a highly literate, at times funny, and always detailed account of his journey across Europe during the downfall of the first Empire.

WRITING THE DIARY

Fernando spent his time in England perfecting his English, working in the commercial house of Gordon and Murphy, and meeting Joseph's friends. One of the most important in Fernando's life was Louisa Moore, daughter of James Moore and the niece of Sir John Moore, the

British general killed at the Battle of Corunna in 1809. The Moores had embraced Joseph when he settled in London; Fernando and Ferdinand, Joseph's son, would also find themselves welcomed as part of the family.[42] Comments in the diary and subsequent letters from Joseph and Ferdinand suggest that Fernando and Louisa formed a sentimental attachment during this period, despite the fact that in 1815, Louisa was only thirteen years old and Fernando was twenty-nine. The reader of the diary will find mentions of a "friend" with whom and to whom he is writing the account of his flight. There are also affectionate outbursts, which might be intended for this friend. For example, when recounting his crossing of the English Channel from Holland, he reflected on his conversation with English passengers and his love of certain expressions, heartfelt if not idiomatic: "I then heard for the first time that tender manner in the English language of calling *things* to animate beings. I never have forgotten it and have made use of it in my most fond moments. It conveys a great meaning to my heart. For instance, I could not say a more fond expression to a woman than *sweet little thing for love.* I leave English ears to judge of the exactness of the expression but as for my meaning if I was to make a language of my own I could not express it better than with this words as I feel them." The flirtatiousness and affection of the passage are unmistakable.

More evidence of his connection to Louisa and perhaps of her role in the writing of the diary comes from letters written to Fernando after his return to Spain, including Joseph's, in which he informed Fernando that he was sending him his books and papers left with the Moores. Ferdinand White stayed with the Moores many years later when he was on leave from military service in India.[43] A letter from Ferdinand to his uncle contained a long, affectionate note from Louisa.

> My dear friend Ferdinand [Fernando]: I think I see your look of surprise at opening this sheet. "A letter from Louisa, containing too the handwriting of my nephew!" Truly I rejoice to say, we have le petit Ferdinand domesticated among us; and I

> suggested to him to write with me a joint letter to you. Happy shall I be if I am able to rouse to an answer.[44] I have written two or three times to you, and countless are the times I think of you, and read over your letters of 1815 and 16 when I was a child, while, now I am descending fast into an old Woman, but I retain all the feelings of younger days; and this youth that I am going immediately to talk to you about, has brushed up my memory of older times.

After recounting the family's exploits in the two decades since he had left England, Louisa concluded her note: "I hope that your Wife, my dear Ferdinand is well in health, and in a manner resigned to the sad losses you have sustained, it will give me sincere pleasure to learn that you are well and prospering. I heard that you have had sad vexation with Business, and would like to know that this has ceased. God bless you, Dear friend of my Youth Gone. Believe me affectionately your Nina de Londres." Ferdinand added his own affectionate comment about "your 'charming little girl' of former days," who had been such a friend to him over many years.[45]

While this textual and epistolary evidence is indirect, I do believe that it allows us to speculate that Louisa played an important role in the writing of Fernando's diary, as a reader, editor, and amanuensis, and as a recommender of readings that Fernando might take as models for his own work.[46] Perhaps most importantly, she was the muse who inspired him to write the account in the first place, the "other" to whom he addressed his autobiographical writing. As Ángel Loureiro has observed, "any autobiographical statement is a response to an other that demands that one explain oneself."[47] In addition to this intimate dimension of the diary, Louisa might have played a role in introducing Fernando to the great wave of British writing about the Peninsular War and other military theaters in the protracted conflict with Napoleonic France. If Fernando ever intended to publish his account, it would have fit well into this British vogue for military reminiscences.[48] At the same time, Louisa's presence in the diary might also indicate one reason why Fernando never published it (if he ever intended to do so): as a married man in Seville, the hints of a connection to a young English girl could hardly have pleased his wife and family.[49]

Fernando's fraternal connection to Joseph, who also likely took part in editing the diary (judging from several marginal comments in Spanish), might also explain why the diary went unpublished. Once he returned to the conservative milieu of Seville under the restoration, Fernando, while deeply attached to Joseph, no doubt had to play down his role as brother of Spain's most famous and reviled expatriate. Conservatives despised the religious apostate, while liberals still smarted from the sharp criticisms made in *El Español*, which some of them considered nothing short of treasonous.[50] During Spain's Liberal Triennium (1820–23), when a military uprising forced Ferdinand VII to accept the Constitution of Cádiz until a French invasion restored the absolutist order, Joseph himself warned Fernando about this lingering animosity and said that he would refrain from publishing political commentary in Spanish because of its potentially negative consequences for his brother and his family.

> Though I am in hopes that the present political storm will blow over, yet I consider the state of that country so ill settled as to imagine that there may arise a combination of circumstances in which I might be urged to write in favor of a limited Constitutional Monarchy according to my well known principles. There is not, however, the most remote chance of that event, for the present; and I confess that I should decline the task as long as it might be consistent with my duty. Yet I wish to know whether entering again the political lists would endanger your peace and quiet; for if you conceive that any odium or suspicion might attach to you, I would do every thing in my power to remain in the absolute silence which I have preserved since 1814. I repeat that there is not the least reason to suppose that my pen will again be exerted in the cause of Spain.[51]

The great hatred that many Spaniards, from the left and the right, felt for his brother likely disinclined Fernando from calling attention to his own exploits during Spain's War of Independence and its immediate aftermath.

In considering how the diary is organized and narrated, I believe it is useful to consider it as a form of travel writing, though it is important to remember that "soldiers were no ordinary travellers."[52] My initial hunch was that Fernando might have based his work on famous Spanish accounts of captivity and flight, such as Alvar Núñez Cabeza de Vaca's *Naufragios* or Miguel de Cervantes's novel within the novel about a captive who escapes from Algiers.[53] Indeed, there are parallels to those works, including the emphasis on "novelty, confusion, and disorder" and the sense of "the world turned upside down," though, as we will see, Fernando and his companions' efforts to maintain social distinctions and rank was firm even in the greatest moments of disorientation.[54] However, Fernando's literary points of reference indicate more familiarity with British travel writing from the Grand Tour, perhaps acquired under the influence of Louisa and the Moore family. The diary makes reference to at least one British travel writer, Lady Mary Wortley Montagu, who made some rather sharp comments on the Catholic churches of Cologne and the Rhineland in letters written during her journey across the Continent in the early eighteenth century—anticlerical sentiments that Fernando echoed. His diary contains many of the elements that scholars have identified as typical of such writings in the eighteenth and early nineteenth centuries: the figure of the "suffering traveler," enlightened descriptions of the towns and customs he encountered, an emphasis on the picturesque, and an exploration of the relationship between the exterior world and interior feelings, in Fernando's case usually expressed as melancholy.[55] He indicated his familiarity with these works and their implications when he commented, somewhat ironically, on a horse medicine provided by a physician in Frankfurt: "thus by traveling is knowledge spread."[56]

The origins of this genre were in the Grand Tour, which peaked in popularity in the era before the French Revolution. Young upper-class British men finished their education by traveling on the Continent, with France and Italy being the key destinations. During the protracted wars with France, when a tour of Europe was almost impossible except for soldiers, aristocratic travelers instead turned their attention the British Isles; the Lake District and the Celtic fringe became destinations and objects of travel writing. Here, of course, we see the major distinction between Fernando and the authors of the works he emulated. His travel was not intended to refine his education but to secure his freedom, and he traveled not in luxury but in harsh and uncomfortable conditions on foot, as well as in carts, sleds, and

Naval Officers and a Bowl of Punch, by Thomas Rowlandson (1756–1827). (Yale Center for British Art, Paul Mellon Collection)

a charabanc (a carriage with several rows of benches) that he and the Porres brothers purchased in Freiburg.[57]

Nonetheless, Fernando's work shares important characteristics with these aristocratic and luxurious precedents and with other travel writers: "a focus on the centrality of the self, a concern with empirical detail, and a movement through time and place which is simply sequential."[58] What do we learn of the self that Fernando revealed in this work? We learn that he loved punch and, especially in the latter phases of his journey, would seek out an inn or pub that served it after a day's travel.[59] He loved music, one of the comforts of his captivity and a passion that he shared with Joseph. He was curious and enlightened, as his desire to study in Paris demonstrates, though he admitted that he was not enlightened enough to overcome deep Spanish prejudices, especially hating Jews, as he recounted when he lodged with a Jewish family in Ettenheim: "Can prejudices have such power even upon *enlightened* minds! I must acknowledge that the idea of being among Jews made me uncomfortable, tho' they were the most excellent people."[60] He tried to teach himself German during the journey and conversed in several languages on the road, including Latin with a cathedral canon (the position held by Joseph before fleeing Spain). His comments on the cities and countryside through which he passed, descriptive in the manner of travel writing, demonstrated a strong taste for neoclassical architecture and planning, dislike for the gothic or that which was simply old, anticlericalism, and interest in economic improvement. (See his contrasting remarks on Catholic Cologne and Protestant Düsseldorf.) Perhaps he summed up the self presented to his (few) readers most concisely when he called himself "a philosopher," able to resist the vicious behavior to which his companions occasionally fell prey and to observe all around him.[61]

LIBERTY AND SLAVERY

In addition to what Fernando revealed about himself and showed about conditions in the crumbling Napoleonic Empire, there are several interesting themes that cut across his diary. Among them are the condition of liberty (and its negation), honor and masculinity, and the possibility of concord, or renewed conflict, among Spaniards after the defeat of France and its collaborators.

On several occasions, Fernando fretted about his vulnerability and the possibility of again losing his liberty. Right at the beginning of his flight, when allied forces in the neighborhood received him and his companions, he criticized the carelessness of the Austrian commander for "having exposed our liberty" by mistakenly sending them to Louhans, where they were menaced by a French mob.[62] And at the end of his journey, when the English shore hove into view, he rejoiced at his arrival to the land that was to be the "shelter for my liberty."[63] His preoccupation with liberty reflected the proximate experience of captivity and the fear that accompanied him on his long, unpredictable flight from France. Indeed, he practically frames the diary as a narrative of liberty vindicated and enslavement overcome. He and his companions were obsessed with "breaking their chains." As French power crumbled, a sympathetic local urged them to throw off the "fers de Napoleon" and flee to the approaching allies.[64]

In a broader framework, Fernando's concerns also spoke to the changes that were taking place in Spanish political life during the struggle against France. Though Fernando spent much of the war as a prisoner, he was home for the heady days of the early Spanish resistance and the ebullience that accompanied it. He had fought to defend his country and, we can infer, its liberation.

What did an educated Spaniard like Fernando mean by *liberty* and its negation, *slavery*? As a European who had never traveled beyond the Continent, his conception of this dichotomy was distinct from that of American contemporaries, many of whom were also struggling to affirm their liberty, and to rid their lands of slavery. For Fernando, *slavery* did not connote the transatlantic traffic and the sugar plantations of Cuba and other American colonies; rather, it referred to the condition of Spaniards under the absolutist monarchies of the Habsburgs and the Bourbons. The imposition of absolutism had deprived the Spaniards of historic liberties and made them dependent upon the benevolence and caprices of the monarchy. Unable to govern themselves, Spanish "vassals" fell into a form of dependent servitude. Such a condition was especially acute during the final years of the reign of Charles IV, when the favorite, Manuel Godoy, ruled the court and the country capriciously, enriching himself at the expense of the king's vassals.[65]

The overthrow of the Bourbons in 1808 and the rising against the French created the opportunity to reclaim ancient liberties and to abolish the servitude under which Spaniards had suffered for almost three hundred years. Vassalage would be abolished and citizenship would take its place, based upon individual freedom and, for certain sectors of society (male and propertied), political equality. In the war-torn years of the Cortes of Cádiz (1810–14), political opponents divided into so-called *liberales*, who defended constitutional monarchy and popular sovereignty, and *serviles*, who wished to return to the absolutist order and who rallied to Ferdinand VII upon his return to the country after the French evacuation.[66]

Fernando's experience of captivity was thus the antithesis of the liberty that he and other Spanish liberals affirmed and defended against the French and against Spanish *serviles*. He was at the mercy of his captors and dependent for his livelihood upon his distant family. His description of French prisoners encountered on his sojourn through the Rhineland spoke eloquently to his own experience: "A prisoner is a very wretched thing even with the hopes of getting liberty. I saw it now in the impatience of these poor French, particularly in those who had been stript of all their property, that's to say, of all that they had plundered in Spain, for they had nothing else."[67] Coerced, deprived of wealth, dependent upon the will of others: such was the slavery that Fernando had endured and from which he sought to escape forever.

Fernando's reflections on liberty and slavery fit within the Spanish and European framework, but his brother Joseph expanded their meanings as he pondered the plight of Fernando and thousands of other Spaniards. He considered how it might be made to resemble the Atlantic and American situation, of which he learned more in his British exile.[68] Scholars of early Spanish liberalism during the Cortes of Cádiz have sought to explain how a liberal, constitutional regime could reconcile itself to colonial slavery and to a political order that explicitly excluded free people of color from active political citizenship.[69] Among the factors were political calculation to preserve peninsular predominance in the elected body in spite of the numerical superiority of the colonial population; appeasement of the powerful Havana planter class, which sought to promote a plantation revolution in Cuba; and old regime prejudices, which, as we have seen, equated dependence with servility. Thus, metropolitan revolutionaries cast free people of color in the colonies as unfit for active citizenship because they continued to bear, even in their freedom, the stigma of slavery.[70]

In contrast to his many peninsular peers, who justified slavery and racial exclusion, Joseph sought to equate the condition of captive Spaniards and enslaved Africans. His friendships and reliance upon abolitionists and reformers in London introduced him to a political and ideological milieu quite different from that of Seville, Madrid, and Cádiz, the Spanish cities in which he lived before his flight to England in 1810. Until the early nineteenth century, Britain was the major carrier in the transatlantic slave trade, in sharp contrast to Spain, which had historically relied upon provision of enslaved Africans to its colonies by foreign merchants, who bid for monopoly contracts. But in the years surrounding the French invasion of the Iberian Peninsula, Britain and Spain were reversing courses. Spanish planters and officials, envious of the great plantation wealth of Jamaica and Saint-Domingue, opted for an unregulated slave trade at the end of the eighteenth century, with Cuba as the major destination. In dramatic contrast, Britain saw the emergence of a mass antislavery movement that demanded the suppression of the slave traffic. Though its fortunes waxed and waned in the era of the French Revolution and the Napoleonic wars, the antislavery movement soon achieved victory when the British parliament abolished the slave trade to the British colonies in 1807.[71]

Joseph adapted quickly to this environment, influenced no doubt by the patronage of Lord Holland, his acquaintance with premier abolitionist William Wilberforce, and his attraction to the evangelical Christianity that animated Wilberforce and thousands of other antislavery proponents.[72] He incorporated abolitionist articles into his newspaper, *El Español.* More ambitiously, he agreed to translate into Spanish one of Wilberforce's antislavery works, the *Letter on the Abolition of the Slave Trade* (1807). As Joseph effectively rewrote and inflected large sections of the work, he placed great emphasis precisely on the condition that his brother and thousands of Spaniards knew at first hand: captivity. African slaves were prisoners of war, victims of the unscrupulous manipulations of European merchants. They were taken violently from their families and homelands, their fate unknown and unpredictable. The parallel, in his rendering, to the plight of the Spanish prisoners, was only too obvious: "The same blood runs in their veins that runs in yours. The tears that their eyes shed are just like yours. Like you, they are parents, children, and siblings. . . . You, who know what it is to have [your families] ripped from your homes by foreign soldiers, leave to the father his children, and to the husband his wife."[73]

HONOR AND MASCULINITY

As soon as Fernando grasped for liberty, concern with his honor rose to the fore. Honor was certainly related to the questions of liberty and slavery, as a man of honor and noble status like Fernando would expect to take an active role in the republic under the conditions of freedom. The prisoner, like the slave, was in practice degraded because of his dependence and his inability to exercise his will freely. He bore the stigma of his condition and was despised because of it. Encountering French captives in the Rhineland, Fernando wrote, "I remembered how most of the French had insulted my misery, and how humiliated they were now."[74]

Escape provoked a crisis because he was breaking his word of honor (*parole d'honneur*) that he would not attempt flight from captivity.[75]

Such a promise was standard in European warfare in the eighteenth and into the early nineteenth centuries. Officers taken prisoner could give their word of honor that they would refrain from fighting against their captors. In exchange, they were free to return to their homes in many cases. For example, after a resounding British victory over French armies at Vimeiro in Portugal in 1808, British officials agreed to ship back to France men and materiel at British expense. The Convention of Sintra, as this agreement was called, was, however, controversial in Britain because it did not even include the provision that Marshal Jean-Andoche Junot's army refrain from fighting in Spain and Portugal after its repatriation.[76] Fernando's situation differed in important ways because the prisoners captured during the French rout of Spanish armies were deported to France. Since the breakdown of the short-lived Peace of Amiens (1802), France, in light of its overwhelming battlefield successes, held on to thousands of Austrian, Russian, and, after 1808, Spanish prisoners rather than exchanging them or allowing them to return home. Fernando found himself trapped in this situation. When he and other officers gave their word of honor, it was not in order to be returned to Spain but to be allowed to live outside of the barracks and to receive benefits from the French state and from their families. In exchange, they would not try to escape their imprisonment.[77]

However, Fernando insisted in his diary that even though he appeared to have broken his word by escaping, he remained "full of honour" because in truth, it was the French who had violated the terms of the agreement from the very first moment. He explained the captors' duplicity in great detail to justify his behavior, perhaps to himself and most certainly to his friend Louisa Moore. The French government had repeatedly cheated them (though he does not spell out how) and had violated the principle of the agreement by forcing the captive officers to attend roll calls on a daily basis, thus implicitly distrusting and dismissing the officers' honor. More seriously, the government had coerced them into giving false information so as to reduce its financial commitment to them.

> But the greatest argument in our favour is the forgery committed in the act of taking our signatures by the *treacherous government* of Bonaparte, for in the beginning of our engagement where our names, rank, and qualities were written, they inscribed every one in a military degree lower than his own, in order to ascertain afterward that we had signed to be only of that rank. Many a one signed without reading. Some read it and asked to be qualified with their own ranks, but they answered them to sign it in that way if they did not like to be shut in a fortress. Others did not agree to sign it and were sent to the fortress in Flanders. The purpose on which this was done was still more horrid, for it was to avoid any further reclamation of our full pay, which they had already lessened to every one to a degree lower. After this it is impossible to find a single person who would think valid this kind of engagement where the French government was only endeavouring to cheat us.[78]

Another way in which Fernando strove to demonstrate his honor, most likely with his friend Louisa in mind, was through his description of his interactions with women along his trek to freedom. Rather than engaging in the boastful, swaggering tone of conquests and prowess, as was often to be found in the construction of military masculinity in this era,[79] Fernando instead emphasized his restraint in the face of temptation, contrasting his behavior with that of some of the acquaintances he made during his journey. For example, in Bern, he was struck by the officially sanctioned brothel, which led him to remark on the difference between the passions satisfied there and the implicit affection for his "friend": "It is to be sure a horrid thing to think, that such places exist in the world, yet it must be owned that many evils are prevented by them. What distance, great God, between the riotous scenes in those places, and the sweet intercourse of two tender virtuous lovers! Yet the former is but the corruption of the latter. To what depravity will not man arrive!"[80] He reiterated his restraint and honor when recounting his prolonged stay in Freiburg with French émigrés.

During the several weeks spent there while one of the Porres brothers recuperated from an illness, he befriended Mademoiselle Corbier, with whom he took long walks and spoke at length about his captivity.

> There I walked with an unmarried lady thro' woods and over without being in the least a subject for scandal. I observed to her sometimes the apparent impropriety of our walks. Why, answered she, I would not do it in France because the manners don't allow it, but I assure you that everywhere I will trust a gentleman, and that I feel as secure by your side as I would do by my Father's. That you may, said I, for no man of feeling would dare abuse such a confidence. This was so true that I never felt the least temptation, even to take of her hand.[81]

SPANIARDS

Fernando's concern with liberty and honor were intimately connected to his sense of social standing and distinction as a Spaniard of noble rank. Yet those distinctions did not cut him off from other captives who came from different strata of society, especially in the context of war, captivity, and flight. A sense of camaraderie with Spaniards of other social stations emerges in his diary. In other words, apparent in his pages is some feeling of national belonging, a topic that has engendered important debates in Spanish historiography in recent years.

In the nineteenth century, though Spanish liberals and conservatives disagreed about how to commemorate the War of Independence against France, both saw it as a moment of national resurgence, when the people joined together to expel the foreign intruders. On the left, the war was seen as an affirmation of liberty; on the right, as a defense of the monarchy and religion. Either way, it was a founding moment in the efforts to define and narrate the national history in the modern era. More recently, historians have committed themselves to debunking the myths around the war. They have argued that the very sobriquet of the war placed a coherent framework upon inchoate events for explicitly political ends. Moreover, they have called into question the idea of a people in arms by scrutinizing the motives and efficacy of the best-known combatants, the Spanish *guerrilleros*. Rather than expressing a strong national identity, the *guerrilleros* fought for largely local interests, which varied greatly across the peninsula. Moreover, some argue that Wellington's Anglo-Portuguese army was the principal nemesis of Napoleon's forces, not the *guerrilla*. These points are among the arguments that historians now adduce to question whether the war crystallized national sentiment.[82]

Nonetheless, there is important evidence to be gleaned from Fernando's diary that suggests why in the nineteenth century some Spaniards might indeed have seen the war in its various aspects as a crucible in which a stronger sense of national unity was forged. Especially interesting is that Fernando, and later his brother, was commenting on feelings and encounters far from Spain, amid the unstable community of prisoners and exiles.[83] Though Fernando was far from home, Spain and Spaniards were ever present during his trek. Along his route, he and his companions met other escapees (including the many gathered at the continental terminus in the Netherlands); they also encountered soldiers released from the depots to work as laborers in the French countryside. Such was the case when a man whom Fernando took to be a French peasant exclaimed to his workmate, "Chico, estos son españoles!" Some would join up with them. In addition to these happy scenes of recognition were the frequent, and sometimes tense, encounters with travelers on a reverse course. Frenchmen, Germans, Swiss, and Hollanders were coming *from* Spain, where they had served the occupying army as soldiers and workers.[84] On January 13, for example, the Spanish fugitives met in Champagnole French deserters whose "pockets were filled with Spanish gold and silver . . . the whole was but the fruit of their robberies in Spain." In several places in his diary, Fernando noted how Spaniards tried to band together in spite of clear-cut regional and class distinctions, as when his group of Andalusian gentlemen welcomed into their midst a Catalan escapee and his young son: "We were yet supping when a

Spanish officer named Tolrá with his son 12 years old joined us. This man was a Catalonian of the lowest description yet, besides his rough manners, a very respectable man. He made his escape with his young boy in the same manner we did and this child followed him always walking. Although we did not *know* him, we admitted him in our company for being a Spaniard."[85]

Several years later, Joseph would reflect upon exactly these encounters described by his brother when he argued in a British periodical that the war had indeed strengthened national sentiment, especially among those forced into exile and captivity: "Many thousands of prisoners from every part of Spain were kept together in the great depôts of Dijon and Chalon sur Saône; and, though, even in that state of durance, the fanciful provincial distinctions were not entirely neglected by the prisoners, the contact was too close not to overcome the mutual repulsion at least in a great degree. We do not speak from conjecture: we know these facts through a highly educated Spanish officer, who was in that depôt four years."[86] At the same time, Fernando's frequent meetings on the road with his countrymen who had served Napoleon and Joseph I presaged the rancorous divisions that opened after Ferdinand VII's restoration. For example, when he found himself among the huge numbers of Spaniards gathered on the Dutch coast, awaiting embarkation for England, Fernando and his fellow officers had to expel from their shelter a "bad Spaniard," most likely a collaborator: "We came back to our companions whom we found very busy about one of the bad Spaniards who wanted to live among us. He was notified to quit immediately before we came to ruder means."[87] Thus, even as regional and class distinctions proved superable in the crucible of captivity and flight, new divisions and loyalties, forged in the conditions of war, resistance, and collaboration would divide Spaniards against one another, not only on the long road home (which some would never reach) but also right in the heart of Spain.

NOTES

1. Vicente Llorens, *Liberales y románticos: Una emigración española en Inglaterra (1823–1834)*, 3rd ed. (Valencia: Castalia, 1979).

2. There are now numerous biographies of Joseph Blanco White, as well as several editions of his autobiographical writings, but the most outstanding is by Martin Murphy. It makes wide use of the Princeton collection, in addition to the other large holdings of Blanco White papers in Oxford and Liverpool. See Martin Murphy, *Blanco White: Self-Banished Spaniard* (New Haven: Yale University Press, 1989). On Blanco as an autobiographer, see James D. Fernández, *Apology to Apostrophe: Autobiography and the Rhetoric of Self-Representation in Spain* (Durham: Duke University Press, 1992), and Ángel Loureiro, *The Ethics of Autobiography: Replacing the Subject in Modern Spain* (Nashville: Vanderbilt University Press, 2000).

3. On this phase of Blanco White's career, the indispensable works are André Pons, *Blanco White y España* (Oviedo: Instituto Feijoo de Estudios del Siglo XVIII, 2002), and *Blanco White y América* (Oviedo: Instituto Feijoo de Estudios del Siglo XVIII, 2006).

4. See Joselyn M. Almeida, *Reimagining the Transatlantic, 1780–1890* (Burlington, VT: Ashgate, 2011), 105–50; and Manuel Moreno Alonso, *La forja del liberalismo en España: Los amigos españoles de Lord Holland, 1793–1840* (Madrid: Publicaciones del Congreso de los Diputados, 1997).

5. Joseph's religious life is a major theme in Murphy, *Blanco White*; Loureiro, *Ethics of Autobiography*, chap. 2; and Fernando Durán López, *José María Blanco White, o la conciencia errante* (Seville: Fundación José Manuel Lara, 2005).

6. Joseph Blanco White, *The Life of the Rev. Joseph Blanco White, written by himself: with portions of his correspondence*, 3 vols., ed. John Hamilton Thom (London: John Chapman, 1845), 1:3.

7. Blanco White, *Life of the Rev. Joseph Blanco White*, 1:4. Fernando's military service record stated his condition as "noble." See Archivo General Militar de Segovia (hereafter AGMS), first section, legajo B-3103.

8. Blanco White, *Life of the Rev. Joseph Blanco White*, 1:5.

9. One of the principals, Col. Juan Murphy, was also a Spaniard of Irish origin. On his family and business, particularly with Mexico, see Martin Murphy, "The Murphys of Waterford, Málaga, Mexico and London," *Irish Genealogist* 13, no. 3 (2012): 210–11.

10. See the lengthy letter that he wrote about a month after arriving in England: London, April 23, 1814, Blanco White Family Collection (hereafter BWFC), 1713–1930 (mostly 1798–1841), Manuscripts Division, Department of Rare Books and Special Collections, Princeton University Library, box 9, folder 6.

11. Certificates of his purification can be found in the service record in the AGMS

and in BWFC, box 14, folder 3, dated Cádiz, May 26, 1816. Fernando describes his encounter with a Freemason in a pub in Soleure on January 20, 1814. On Fernando and Freemasonry in France, his brother Joseph wrote in a letter many years later: "Our Uncle who rose to high degrees in France, and was in danger on that account on his return to Spain, spoke to me very highly of the institution." Letter to Ferdinand White, dated Liverpool, April 2, 1836, Joseph Blanco White Collection, Liverpool University (hereafter JBWC/LU), Special Collections and Archives BW 141. My thanks to Martin Murphy for sharing this letter with me. On Freemasonry in the depots, see Jean René Aymes, *Los españoles en Francia, 1808–1814: La deportación bajo el Primer Imperio* (Madrid: Siglo XXI, 1987), 205–13.

12. On Fernando's career as an educator, see the copy of his curriculum vita dated Seville, March 27, 1848, in BWFC, box 14, folder 4. On his public service during the tempestuous Liberal Triennium, see the letter to Joseph dated Seville, July 2, 1823, Blanco White Papers, Manuscript Collection, Harris Manchester College, Oxford (hereafter BWP/HMC), section 1, folios 14–15.

13. Fernando White to Joseph Blanco White, dated Seville, April 7, 1819, JBWC/LU, BW 1/2. My thanks to Joselyn M. Almeida for sharing this letter with me. For a more extensive discussion of the family's economic situation, see Murphy, *Blanco White.*

14. Ferdinand White to Fernando, dated Chatham, July 10, 1839, BWFC, box 9, folder 4.

15. BWFC, box 17, folder 12.

16. Blanco White, *Life of the Rev. Joseph Blanco White,* 1:50. Loureiro shows that a constant theme across Joseph's many autobiographical writings was his liberation from that enslavement. See Loureiro, *Ethics of Autobiography,* chap. 2.

17. A recent treatment of the larger interests implicated in the Spanish court's conflicts and the French responses is Barbara H. Stein and Stanley J. Stein, *Crisis in an Atlantic Empire: Spain and New Spain, 1808–1810* (Baltimore: Johns Hopkins University Press, 2014).

18. See Esdaile, *The Peninsular War: A New History* (London: Allen Lane, 2002), chaps. 1–5.

19. On the political struggles within Spain, see Stein and Stein, *Crisis in an Atlantic Empire.* On Seville during the Napoleonic era, see Manuel Moreno Alonso, *Sevilla napoleónica* (Seville: Ediciones Alfar, 1995), and Charles Esdaile, *Outpost of Empire: Napoleonic Occupation of Andalusia, 1810–1812* (Norman: University of Oklahoma Press, 2012).

20. Fernando Blanco White to Guillermo Blanco y Morrogh, dated Madrid, November 29, 1808, BWFC, box 9, folder 3.

21. Fernando Blanco White to Guillermo Blanco y Morrogh and María Gertrudis Crespo y Neve, dated Moulins, February 10, 1809, BWFC, box 9, folder 6.

22. Fernando Blanco White to Guillermo Blanco y Morrogh and María Gertrudis Crespo y Neve, dated Dijon, February 28, 1810, BWFC, box 7, folder 4.

23. On the experience of captivity during the revolutionary wars of the era, both in Europe and the colonial world, see Aymes, *Los españoles en Francia;* Linda Colley, *Captives: Britain, Empire, and the World, 1600–1850* (New York: Pantheon, 2002), chap. 7; Michael Lewis, *Napoleon and His British Captives* (London: Allen and Unwin, 1962); Denis Smith, *The Prisoners of Cabrera: Napoleon's Forgotten Soldiers, 1809–1814* (New York: Four Walls Eight Windows, 2001); Edwin G. Burrows, *Forgotten Patriots: The Untold Story of American Prisoners during the Revolutionary Wars* (New York: Basic Books, 2008); Catriona Kennedy, *Narratives of the Revolutionary and Napoleonic Wars: Military and Civilian Experience in Britain and Ireland* (New York: Palgrave Macmillan, 2013), chap. 5; and Christopher Schmidt-Nowara, "Spanish Prisoners: War and Captivity in Spain's Imperial Crisis, 1808–1824," in *Empire's End: Transnational Connections in the Hispanic World, 1808–1898*, ed. William Acree and Akiko Tsuchiya (Nashville: Vanderbilt University Press, 2016).

24. See the discussion in Aymes, *Los españoles en Francia,* 147–49.

25. Fernando Blanco White to Guillermo Blanco y Morrogh, dated Chalon SS, November 10, 1812, BWFC, box 9, folder 6. The fortress of Joux was where Toussaint Louverture died in 1803 after his imprisonment by Napoleon. Fernando makes no mention of him but describes the fortress, on the border with Switzerland, during his flight from France on January 14–15. By that time it had fallen to the Austrians. Maestre, like Fernando, was a volunteer from Seville. He was captured at the Battle of Somosierra in 1808. According to his service record, the Spanish crown recognized his attempts to escape with a medal given to "the prisoners who were held in the French castles or who had escaped from them." See AGMS, first section, legajo M-137.

26. Fernando Blanco White to Guillermo Blanco y Morrogh, dated Dijon, July 17, 1810, BWFC, box 9, folder 5.

27. Fernando Blanco White to Guillermo Blanco y Morrogh, dated Dijon, February 28, 1810, BWFC, box 7, folder 4.

28. A letter to his father dated Chalon SS, January 1813, makes note of Guillermo having repaid a loan to the parents of Juan María Maestre. BWFC, box 9, folder 6.

29. Mention of "slavery" and of Joseph's help in restoring his monetary transfers, in Fernando Blanco White to Guillermo Blanco y Morrogh, dated Chalon SS, January 1813, BWFC, box 9, folder 6. He mentions his "humiliations" in letters dated Chalon SS, August 17 and October 14, 1813, BWFC, box 9, folder 6.

30. Fernando Blanco White to Guillermo Blanco y Morrogh, dated Dijon, April 8, 1810, BWFC, box 9, folder 6.

31. Fernando Blanco White to Guillermo Blanco y Morrogh, dated Chalon SS, 20 October 1811, BWFC, box 9, folder 6.

32. Ibid.

33. Aymes, *Los españoles en Francia*, chap. 5. See also Lewis, *Napoleon and His British Captives*, chap. 2; and Kennedy, *Narratives of the Revolutionary and Napoleonic Wars*, chap. 5.

34. Archivo Histórico Nacional (Madrid), Sección de Estado (hereafter AHN/E), legajo, 5936, dispatch no. 75, Langres, February 1, 1814. For a recent treatment of the *afrancesados* in the framework of numerous other Spanish and European exile groups, see Juan Luis Simal, *Emigrados: España y el exilio international, 1814–1834* (Madrid: Centro de Estudios Políticos y Constitucionales, 2012). The classic study is Miguel Artola, *Los afrancesados* (1953; Madrid: Alianza, 1989); more recently, see Juan López Tobar, *Los famosos traidores: Los afrancesados durante la crisis del Antiguo Régimen (1808–1833)* (Madrid: Biblioteca Nueva, 2001). On the Alexander Regiment, Spanish POWs who had invaded Russia with Napoleon but then changed sides and served the Russians until 1813, see Richard Stites, *The Four Horsemen: Riding to Liberty in Post-Napoleonic Europe* (New York: Oxford University Press, 2014), 56.

35. Aymes, *Los españoles en Francia*, 111.

36. AHN/E, legajo 5936, dispatch no. 52, Basel, January 16, 1814.

37. AHN/E, legajo 5936, dispatch no. 87, Châtillon-sur-Seine, February 10, 1814.

38. AHN/E, legajo 5936, dispatch no. 263, Paris, June 28, 1814. The response of Spain's men on the spot differed from those at the center of the restored monarchy. Pizarro's dispatches, in which he sought financial assistance so that he could offer aid to the ex-prisoners and to Spanish deserters alike, found echoes in those of other Spanish officials along the route from France to England (by way of the Rhineland and the Netherlands). For example, the Spanish minister in London, the Count of Fernán-Núñez, began writing to his government in December 1813, notifying the ministry of the arrival of Spanish escapees and deserters to English ports. He foresaw that this trickle would soon become a flood and asked for monies to relieve them and to have them sent home to Spain. See his dispatches dated London, December 13 and 17, 1813, AHN/E, legajo 5464, dispatches nos. 311 and 315. In other words, Spanish officials on the spot in Europe and England were responsive to the crisis of the refugees regardless of their role in the War of Independence, even if the policies of the soon-to-be-restored monarchy were more suspicious and ultimately divisive. However, it should be noted that Fernando Blanco White responded negatively to his interactions with these officials: "I dislike extremely the coldness with which those who are employed by the Spanish government behave to their countrymen" (Diary, January 22, Basel).

39. On the military history of France's defeat in 1814, see Vincent J. Esposito, *A Military History and Atlas of the Napoleonic Wars* (New York: Praeger, 1964); Charles Esdaile, *The Peninsular War*; and Ralph Ashby, *Napoleon against Great Odds: The Emperor and the Defenders of France, 1814* (Santa Barbara: Praeger, 2010).

40. Guillermo Curtoys, dispatch no. 19, London, June 15, 1814, AHN/E, legajo 5466.

41. See the letter from Joseph to Fernando dated 7 Paradise Row, Chelsea, May 9, 1822, BWFC, box 7, folder 3.

42. Murphy, *Blanco White*, 75.

43. Joseph had purchased an ensignship for him after a brief commercial career came to an end. Ferdinand would serve in Van Diemen's Land and India, and take part in the punitive expedition to sack Kabul after the catastrophe of the First Afghan War. For further information on Ferdinand's extraordinary career, see Martin Murphy's forthcoming biographical essay (personal communication, 2014).

44. Note from Beatrice Forbes Manz and Matthew Ehrlich: Schmidt-Nowara wrote a note to himself to check the original.

45. Letter dated Corswell, Stanraer, August 18, 1838, BWFC, box 9, folder 4. Fernando and his wife Juana lost an infant daughter and their eldest son Guillermo.

46. Scholars have shown that many British women of Louisa's class closely followed and commented on the news of the wars during this era. As the niece of Sir John Moore, Louisa, though young, was perhaps as well informed as any. See Emma V. Macleod, "'Thinking Minds of Both Sexes': Patriotism, British Bluestockings and the Wars against Revolutionary America and France, 1775–1802," in Karen Hagemann, Gisela Mettele, and Jane Rendall, eds., *Gender, War, and Politics: Transatlantic Perspectives, 1775–1830* (New York: Palgrave Macmillan, 2010), 247–64.

47. Loureiro, *Ethics of Autobiography*, xii. For a reflection on the relationship between the author and his muse, see Arcadio Diaz Quiñones, "Introducción," Ramón Emeterio Betances, *Obras completas*, ed. Félix Ojeda Reyes and Paul Estrade (San Juan: Ediciones Puerto, 2008), 2, 25–37, which treats Betances and his beloved niece Lita.

48. Several works have recently drawn upon and explored the dimensions and rhetoric of this body of literature, including unpublished letters and diaries. See Kennedy, *Narratives of the Revolutionary and Napoleonic Wars;* Gavin Daly, *The British Soldier in the Peninsular War: Encounters with Spain and Portugal, 1808–1814* (New York: Palgrave Macmillan, 2013); and Graciela Iglesias Rogers, *British Liberators in the Age of Napoleon: Volunteering under the Spanish Flag in the Peninsular War* (London: Bloomsbury, 2013).

49. Fernando and Louisa did stay in touch with one another when he returned to Seville. An 1823 letter to Joseph contained one for Louisa as well: "You will find enclosed a letter for Louisa Moore. That lovable girl wrote to me last year and it has not been possible for me to answer her until now. The sad fate of this cursed country makes the memory of the happy days that I passed with her affectionate family even more painful." Fernando to Joseph, dated Seville, July 1823, BWP/HMC, section 1, folios 10–11.

50. See Murphy, *Blanco White*, chap. 5, on the angry reactions in Spain to *El Español*. In his *Life*, Joseph recounted that while he edited *El Español*, he always carried

weapons because he feared an assassination attempt ordered from Spain. He wrote that "a letter, in the shape of a friendly warning, and another in the tone of the most sincere Spanish rage, obliged me to purchase a brace of pocket pistols, and to hold one ready when I crossed the solitary fields which lay for about half a mile on the London side of my lodgings" (1:198). Thanks to Joselyn Almeida for calling this anecdote to my attention.

51. Joseph Blanco White to Fernando Blanco White, dated Ufton, Reading, January 6, 1822, BWFC, box 7, folder 3.

52. Daly, *The British Soldier in the Peninsular War,* 214.

53. On the themes of the early modern Spanish captivity narrative, especially in the Mediterranean, see James S. Amelang, "L'autobiografia popolare nella Spagna moderna: Osservazioni generali e particolari," in Giovanni Ciappelli, ed., *Memoria, famiglia, identità tra Italia ed Europa nell'età moderna* (Bologna: Il Mulino, 2009), 113–30. See also María Antonia Garcés, *Cervantes in Algiers: A Captive's Tale* (Nashville: Vanderbilt University Press, 2002); Rolena Adorno and Patrick C. Pautz, *Alvar Núñez Cabeza de Vaca: His Account, His Life, and the Expedition of Pánfilo de Narváez* (Lincoln: University of Nebraska Press, 1999).

54. Amelang, "L'autobiografia popolare," 126.

55. A family trait, according to him. In 1838 he told his brother that he recognized in Ferdinand, Joseph's son, the same disposition: "I perused [Ferdinand's letter] with great pleasure for it breathes that loving melancholy which pervades the blood of the Blanco-Whites." Fernando to Joseph, dated Seville, August 20, 1838, BWP/HMC, section 1, folio 36.

56. Daly, *The British Soldier,* 82; James Buzard, "The Grand Tour and After (1660–1840)," in *The Cambridge Companion to Travel Writing,* ed. Peter Hulme and Tim Youngs (Cambridge: Cambridge University Press, 2002), 37–52; Ana Hontanilla, "Images of Barbaric Spain in Eighteenth-Century British Travel Writing," *Studies in Eighteenth-Century Culture* 37 (2008): 122–23; and John Brewer, "Sentiment and Sensibility," in *The Cambridge History of English Romantic Literature,* ed. James Chandler (Cambridge: Cambridge University Press, 2012), 21–44.

57. Dispatches from the Spanish representatives in England made note of the dire conditions in which the escapees found themselves by the end of their journey. The minister in London, Count Fernán-Núñez, reported that they arrived in "a sad situation of misery and nudity." See dispatch no. 334, dated London, January 4, 1814, AHN/E, legajo 5466. A large contingent of Spanish soldiers arriving in Portsmouth, where they would embark for San Sebastián, were described by the local British commander as "in the most filthy state, almost destitute of covering and many of them very sickly." Copy of letter from Maj. General Brown to the Commander of the Western District, Citadel, Plymouth, January 23, 1814, British National Archives, War Office 1/658.

58. Hulme and Youngs, introduction to *Cambridge Companion to Travel Writing,* 6.

59. The punch party like the one that Fernando and the Porres brothers held in Amsterdam to celebrate suddenly being in the money is the subject of Karen Harvey, "Ritual Encounters: Punch Parties and Masculinity in the Eighteenth Century," *Past and Present* 214, no. 1 (2012): 165–203. The Madrid café-goers in Mariano José de Larra's "El café" (1828) imbibe *ponch.*

60. Diary, February 21. Emphasis in the original.

61. Diary, January 15.

62. Diary, January 9.

63. Diary, March 22.

64. Diary, second page of original, prelude to flight in January.

65. Charles Nicholas Saenz, "Slaves to Tyrants: Social Ordering, Nationhood, and the Constitution of Cadiz of 1812," *Bulletin for Spanish and Portuguese Historical Studies* 37, no. 2 (2012): article 4. On Spanish medievalism in this period, see Brian Hamnett, "The Reception of Romanticism in Italy and Spain: Parallels and Contrasts," *History of European Ideas* 41, no. 2 (2014): 176-89, DOI: 10.1080/01916599.2014.914310. British visitors to the peninsula believed that prerevolutionary Spaniards were "an enslaved People." Quoted in Hontanilla, "Images of Barbaric Spain," 134.

66. Juan Luis Simal, "Más allá de la metáfora: El lenguaje de esclavitud y libertad en el primer liberalismo español," in *Lenguajes de modernidad en la Peninsula Ibérica,* ed. Manuel Pérez Ledesma (Madrid: Universidad Autónoma de Madrid, 2012), 129–30. See also Gabriel Paquette, "Introduction: Liberalism in the Early Nineteenth-Century Iberian World," *History of European Ideas* 41, no. 2 (2014): 153–65, DOI: 10.1080/01916599.2014.914312.

67. Diary, March 4.

68. Christopher Schmidt-Nowara, "Wilberforce Spanished: Joseph Blanco White and Spanish Antislavery, 1808–1814," in *Slavery and Antislavery in Spain's Atlantic Empire,* ed. Josep M. Fradera and Christopher Schmidt-Nowara (New York: Berghahn, 2013), 158–75.

69. Saenz, "Slaves to Tyrants"; Simal, "Más allá de la metáfora"; King, "The Colored Castes and American Representation in the Cortes of Cadiz," *Hispanic American Historical Review* 33 (February 1953): 33–64; Josep M. Fradera, "Raza y ciudadania," *Gobernar colonias (Historia, ciencia, sociedad)* (Barcelona: Ediciones Península, 1999), 51–69; Fradera, "Moments in a Postponed Abolition," in Fradera and Schmidt-Nowara, *Slavery and Antislavery in Spain's Atlantic Empire,* 256–90; Tamar Herzog, *Defining Nations: Immigrants and Citizens in Early Modern Spain and Spanish America* (New Haven: Yale University Press, 2003), chap. 7; and Jeremy Adelman, *Sovereignty and Revolution in the Iberian Atlantic* (Princeton: Princeton University Press, 2006), chap. 2.

70. On this latter point, see in particular Fradera, "Raza y ciudadania," and, more recently, Simal, "Más allá de la metáfora," 136; Simal, *Emigrados,* 45–60; and Saenz, "Slaves to Tyrants," 1–4.

It must be noted that the Spanish Empire was far from unique in drawing this implicit, sometimes explicit, distinction between metropolitan liberty and colonial servitude. Indeed, historians have argued that it was precisely during the revolutionary and Napoleonic eras that a celebratory and triumphalist European world view crystallized and justified a new wave of global expansion and despotic rule over the course of the nineteenth century. See Stuart Woolf, "The Construction of a European World-View in the Revolutionary-Napoleonic Years," *Past & Present* 137 (November 1992): 72–101; Colley, *Captives;* C. A. Bayly, *The Birth of the Modern World, 1780–1914: Global Connections and Comparisons* (Malden, MA: Blackwell, 2004); and John Darwin, *After Tamerlane: The Rise and Fall of Global Empires, 1400–2000* (New York: Bloomsbury, 2008), chaps. 4–6. On how this triumphalist mentality affected the remaining American colonies and successor states in the United States and parts of Latin America, see Fradera, *Gobernar colonias;* Dale Tomich, *Through the Prism of Slavery: Labor, Capital, and World Economy* (Lanham, MD: Rowman and Littlefield, 2004); Rafael de Bivar Marquese and Tâmis Peixoto Parron, "Internacional escravista: A política da Segunda Escravidão," *Topoi* 12 (July–December 2011): 97–117; and Miranda Frances Spieler, *Empire and Underworld: Captivity in French Guiana* (Cambridge, MA: Harvard University Press, 2012).

71. On British abolitionism, see David Brion Davis, *The Problem of Slavery in the Age of Revolution, 1770–1823* (Ithaca: Cornell University Press, 1975); Seymour Drescher, *Capitalism and Antislavery: British Mobilization in Comparative Perspective* (New York: Oxford University Press, 1987); Christopher Leslie Brown, *Moral Capital: Foundations of British Abolitionism* (Chapel Hill: University of North Carolina Press, 2006); and David Ryden, *West Indian Slavery and British Abolition, 1783–1807* (New York: Cambridge University Press, 2009). On changes to the slave trade to Spanish America, see Josep M. Delgado, "The Slave Trade in the Spanish Empire: The Shift from Periphery to Center," in Fradera and Schmidt-Nowara, *Slavery and Antislavery in Spain's Atlantic Empire,* 13–42.

72. On Joseph's experience in London during these years, see Murphy, *Blanco White,* 61–93; and Almeida, *Reimagining the Transatlantic,* 105–50.

73. José María Blanco White, *Bosquejo del comercio de esclavos,* ed. Manuel Moreno Alonso (1814; Seville: Ediciones Alfar, 1999), 195–96.

74. Diary, March 1.

75. The honor system is explained in Lewis, *Napoleon and His British Captives,* chap. 2.

76. On the Convention of Sintra, see Esdaile, *The Peninsular War,* 98–103.

77. See Aymes, *Los españoles en Francia,* 163–68, for a discussion of arrangements in the French depots; and Lewis, *Napoleon and His British Captives,* chap. 2, on changes in French policy toward prisoners of war. Kennedy notes that in retaining British prisoners instead of exchanging them after the failure of the Peace of Amiens, Napoleon

believed that "the French could afford to lose more of their men to imprisonment than the British" (*Narratives of the Revolutionary and Napoleonic Wars*, 116).

78. Diary, January 8.

79. See Alan Forrest, "Citizenship, Honor, and Masculinity: Military Qualities under the French Revolution and Empire," in Hagemann, Mettele, and Rendall, eds., *Gender, War and Politics*, 93–109.

80. Diary, January 19.

81. Diary, January 25–February 21.

82. José Álvarez Junco has been the chief debunker, focusing on historical and political discourse in the mid-nineteenth century. See his "La invención de la Guerra de la Independencia," *Studia Histórica* 12 (1994): 75–99. From the military history perspective, see Esdaile, *The Peninsular War;* John Lawrence Tone, *The Fatal Knot: The Guerrilla War in Navarre and the Defeat of Napoleon in Spain* (Chapel Hill: University of North Carolina Press, 1994); Vittorio Scotti Douglas, "La guerrilla en la Guerra de la Independencia: ¿ayuda imprescindible para la victoria o estorbo grave e inoportuno?" in *La Guerra de la Independencia en Málaga y su provincial (1808–1814)*, ed. Marion Reder Gadow and Eva Mendoza García (Malaga: Servicio de Publicaciones Centro de Ediciones de la Diputación de Málaga, 2005), 63–92; and Ronald Fraser, *Napoleon's Cursed War: Spanish Popular Resistance in the Peninsular War, 1808–1814* (London: Verso, 2008).

83. The role of exiles and transnational networks in shaping European liberalism and nationalism during the age of revolutions is receiving increased attention. See Simal, *Emigrados;* Maurizio Isabella, *Risorgimento in Exile: Italian Émigrés and the Liberal International in Post-Napoleonic Europe* (Oxford: Oxford University Press, 2009); John Davis, "The Spanish Constitution of 1812 and the Mediterranean Revolutions (1820–25)," *Bulletin for Spanish and Portuguese Historical Studies* 37, no. 2 (2012): article 7; Gabriel Paquette, *Imperial Portugal in the Age of Atlantic Revolutions: The Luso-Brazilian World, c. 1770–1850* (Cambridge: Cambridge University Press, 2013), chap. 4; and Henry Kamen, *The Disinherited: Exile and the Making of Spanish Culture, 1492–1975* (New York: HarperCollins, 2007).

84. On collaboration and co-optation in the Napoleonic Empire and military, see Michael Broers, *Europe under Napoleon, 1799–1815* (New York: St. Martin's, 1996).

85. Diary, January 8. Emphasis in the original.

86. Joseph Blanco White, "Inglis's *Spain in 1830*," *Dublin University Review* 2 (November 1834): 303.

87. Diary, March 18.

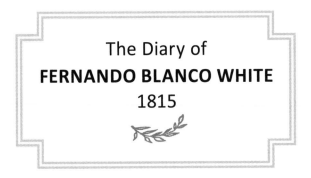

The Diary of

FERNANDO BLANCO WHITE

1815

. . . a prisoner is a very wretched thing even with the hopes of getting liberty.

—March 4th, Siegburg

THO A MAN WHOSE HEART is grateful can not fear to forget the benefits he has received, yet human memory is so slight as to put great confusion in the remembrance of the very same persons to whom we are the more affectionate; thereby I always thought it convenient not to trust to my memory all what have happened to me since my evasion from France, because there are so many good people connected with the events of this journey that it should be very ungrateful if I would not take all precautions for not forgetting their names nor the benefits I owe them.

This work, trifling as it might appear is yet of great consequence to me, therefore I do not think it ridiculous to dedicate it to whom all what concern to me is very interesting. I hope he will read with pleasure this very imperfect sketch of a very tiresome journey even in its description.[1] Nevertheless I am sure he will be affected with the kind reception and hospitality I have met with in some places, tho he may be teased by the dry relation of quite indifferent facts, for I am resolved not to omit the less circumstance. I have undertaken, I know a work above my power, but the genius of my friend will help me in the most arduous of it.[2]

Five years of captivity had tired me in such a manner that I could not see an opportunity of regaining my liberty without embracing it with the greatest eagerness. I had already lost by want of money the

1. Most likely dedicated to his brother Joseph.

2. His friend Louisa Moore. See introduction.

opportunity of fleeing a year and a half before with my best friends: but now the best of all presented itself in the beginning of 1814, that was the approach of the Allied army to Burgundy where I dwelt. All the Spanish officers who were with me in the depot of Chalon S. S. [sur Saône] could not see this event without thinking of breaking their chains by that means, and some of them were as fool as to think it very easy to go openly, all the Officers of the depot, to the Allies who were then a sixty miles from us. I did not apply to those but to the more sensible who wished to have a leader to conduct us in the night through the fields. This was not easy to be found because we did not dare to trust any body, but we find it by a circumstance worthy to be known. One of my friends called Cardenas lived in a Savoyard's house, the greatest enemy of Bonaparte: this good natured man as soon as he knew the proximity of the Allied troops walked to Cardenas' room and in his rude manner said to him. *Quoi. Sac. nom. d. D.* [Sacré nom de Dieu!], *resterez vous comme un lâche dans les fers de Napoleon, pendant que les alliés sont a 18 lieues d'ici? Allons S. n. de D. fis pour le camp de suite.* [In the holy name of God, will you remain here like a coward in Napoleon's irons, when the Allies are 18 leagues from here? In the holy name of God, run to the camp!]

Cardenas answered him that he could not do it because he had no money to pay a guide nor even to pay him his lodgings. Never mind it replied the Savoyard you are a Gentleman and I am sure you will send me everything when you will be in your country; now I shall give you a leader and some little money to do your escape. Cardenas could find no expression to thank the Savoyard for his generosity and repeated to me his astonishing behavior. Cardenas escaped the 5 January and succeeded. I immediately thought to apply to the Savoyard [Desgrange], tho I did not know him. On that purpose one of our party was sent to him. He did no objection to give us his assistance, but finding no body so faithful to lead us as Cardenas' guide thought it proper to wait for his return. He believed we could set off the 6th in the night. All the party was ready but we were disappointed by the guide; then Desgrange caused us to wait till the next day.

Thus disappointed at ten o'clock at night I was obliged to return home and wait till the next day. This inconvenience however procured me a true pleasure, that of knowing how much I was beloved by the girls of the house where I lived: for as in the very moment when I thought I was to set off I left a letter to her mother to let her know which were my intentions—the poor girls could not be ignorant of it, and were very much affeared whether I should not succeed; so that when I came back again I could not but be affected seeing the joy display in their cheeks yet wet with tears. *N'est ce pas que vous ne nous quiteres plus, Mr. Blanco? Qu' aller vous vous exposer?* [You will not leave us anymore will you, Mr. Blanco? Are you going to expose yourself to danger?] These were their words, and I assure that have I not been absolutely decided to break my fetters they would have shook my determination so much was I gratified with their kindness for me.

This night I passed with the utmost tranquility by the only thought of what it should be if I would have begun my journey; but that next day was of great agitation. Some times we thought that everything was ready for our departure, sometimes we believed it impossible. Now we heard the arrival of the guide we were waiting for, was come and that our friends were safe; then we knew that the bridge was occupied and that the town was surrounded by the national guard. That same day two corps of Spanish prisoners arrived at Chalon, and we had orders to be ready to set off with them to the interior of France. Many of my acquaintances came in this two corps, and my house being full of them the whole day, I was obliged to make my preparations before them, concealing at the same time what were my intentions. These moments were very cruel for me for the trouble they gave me and for the uncertainty in which I was.

At six o'clock in the evening nothing was yet certain but we were to meet at the house of one of our companions to wait for the Savoyard. I had but entered the house when one of our party told me in a great hurry; *all is ready, at seven o'clock we set off.* I cannot say what were then my feelings but I know that my agitation was uncommon till the moment when I made the first step in the street. Then I found again my calm [and] I walked with enough serenity. We were ten in all whose names are: Messers Peter, Man.l, and Joseph Porres, all three sons of the Marquis of Castilleja [del Campo] in Seville,[3] my very good friends with whom I have been always since were taken prisoners; Mr. Tadeo Miranda, his chamber fellow Mr. Mariano Gros, both very good natured young men; Mr. Joseph Bidia and his best friend Mr. Antonio Martinez; Mr. Manuel Guevara, cousin to the brothers Porres; Mr. Fontanilles and I. We walked by different ways to the ramparts near the Saône, called of Ste. Marie where the Savoyard, his brother, and the guide were waiting for us at a distance from each other to make us know if there was any danger. *All is right*, they tell us, *step down the ramparts and follow the guide*. We did it so in the greatest silence, and in a moment we were in the fields.

The night was cloudy but not dark because of the moon it fulled a little rays which some times was rather snow [*sic*]; the fields were very wet and muddy, yet we walked so rapidly that we very often passed our guide. His name was Savoje. He conducted us over the right bank of the Saône and walked against the stream for about three miles. There a man named Cretin was waiting for us with a little boat, but so small that he would only take half at once and came back again for the other half. This little *retard* was very useful to Mr. Martinez who forgot near his Love the hour of our departure

3. José de Porres y Ponce de León, the eldest brother, was captured at the fall of Valencia in 1811 and arrived in France in January 1812 (Archivo General Militar de Segovia [AGMS], first section, legajo P-2515). His brother Pedro was captured at Madrid in 1808 (AGMS, first section, legajo P-2516), as was their brother Manuel, who had also taken part in the Battle of Bailén (AGMS, first section, legajo 2515). Pedro was a volunteer like Fernando Blanco White, but José and Manuel were serving in the military before 1808. The North American Hispanist George Ticknor, in the diary that he kept while traveling in Spain in 1818, recounted that in Seville he frequented "the little dances at the Countess of Castillejas [*sic*], which made a more rational amusement than I ever met before at a Spanish tertulia." Rauner Special Collections Library, Dartmouth College, George Ticknor Papers, 1773–1870, series 2, box 2, folder 8, vol. 8. My thanks to Ivan Jaksic for sharing his research on Ticknor with me.

and was obliged to walk alone in the fields till he met us very luckily when the boat was going to pass the second time. This passage was not very easy because the river was overflowed and consequently the stream was very strong.

When we were on the other side we began to cross the fields but there was so much water and so many ditches that very often we had water up to the middle. After having passed the fields we found something worse the ground was ploughed, and our legs sinked till the knees; besides that the jumping across the inclosures was very tiresome. We had good courage against all the inconveniences but soon we lost it when we perceived that the guide did not know where he was. It was ten o'clock when this happened and we were not three miles far from Chalon as it appeared by a farmer to whom the guide applied to inquire his way, whilst we were hid behind an enclosure, and in a great fear of been betraid by him. This poor man did not thought of it, and came over to us seeing that he knew where he was. We continued with a little more confidence tho the guide was obliged to ask again for his way in another country house. Soon after we found a very small road and then the guide told us with very great joy we are in the right way.

Thus we continued till one o'clock in the morning, but we were then so wet, so cold and so hungry that we could not continue without eating something. The difficulty was to find it, and this was not easy because we could be betrayed in the inns as many of our countrymen has been in such cases. Our hunger made us forget all danger and we ventured to get in a little inn which was in the road. The innkeeper was more than a quarter of an hour before he dared open the door and he was not satisfied when he saw eleven young men with all the appearance of foreigners. We only spoke French and affected all the French manners. Half an hour was enough to warm us a little and to take a little bread and cheese with wine and brandy. We said to the innkeeper that we were running away from the Franche Comté because the Allied armies were in our own country. This was very good, but when we were to continue our journey the innkeeper perceived the falsity of our report; so then we were obliged to turn back again like if we were going to Chalon, till the innkeeper shut his door; then we returned in the greatest silence till we passed the inn the strength we got with what we ate encouraged us to run so we did it and we ran three or four miles.

The road beginning to be very bad we could but walk and thus we continued till five o'clock in the morning, always walking in the most horrible dirt I have seen in my life. At this hour the guide told that it was not prudent to continue upon the road, and that the better was to go through the mountains to a little farm where we could pass the following day, and continue in the night our journey. This was approved of because we were extremely tired and cold. We left the road and walked in the woods, but the guide lost his way and wandered in the woods almost exhausted by fatigue about two hours without founding the farm. In this moment I must confess that I lost all my spirits and that I was obliged to make use of all the power of my mind for preventing myself from lying down on the ground. The more the day approached the more our guide was frightened and the less he could find his way. My opinion was to send the guide to a little hill from which he could take some notice of the country. This succeeded because he perceived the farm and conducted us there in less than a quarter of an hour. The farmer was waiting all the night, so he opened immediately, he made fire in this stove, and prepared us a little breakfast. He had but one bed, and the room was so small that we had no place to lie in the ground, so after having walked all the night we were obliged to sit down all the day.[4]

Wet, tired, and hungry as we were yet the confidence we had conceived of succeeding gaved us a great cheerfulness. But this our situation rendered vexatious, for being obliged to be in the greatest silence not to be understood by those who might pass near the house nothing was consequently more provoquing than our great desire of speaking and laughing. Six hours passed in this way till we saw the

4. "Ready" is penciled in at the bottom of the page.

farmer's wife coming a little agitated and tell us: *ces Messieurs n'ont pas voulu que vous vous donniez la peine d'aller les chercher, ils sont venus eux mêmes audevant de vous* [Those gentlemen did not want you to take the trouble of finding them, they have arrived right ahead of you]. What do you mean, cried all; *Que les Autrichiens sont dan le village* [The Austrians are in the village]. Never the arrival of the most beloved friend could make such an impression as this did in our minds. No more silence, no more prudence; every one embraced the others with the greatest transport. To this succeeded very soon the greatest [illegible word] and anxiety, for we observed that we could not go to the village till the night, without exposing the poor farmer to be known in the neighbourhood like a protector of the enemies of his country, and that in the mean time the Allies might turn back again to the corps from which they were only a little detachment, and thus deprive us of such an opportunity of being safe. How slow these hours passed. The poor farmer seeing our generous behavior endeavoured to secure our mind by going every moment to the village to see if what he called the enemy, was still there. At last, as time equally pass in pleasures and in paynes, the night arrived and the moment of our deliverance. Then after having *recompensed* our farmer *Desbois* with three louis d'or we set off with him from his house in the *hameau de la Malporte* to the next village *St. Germain des Bois.*

As we arrived at St. Germain we were very much surprised not to find a single *sentinel*: but very soon we met the whole detachment drinking in a tavern, and soon after the Commander in the house of the Mayor. This officer was an Austrian captain of Hungarian Huzzars of Blanchestein. He could speak very *little* French, and as he was smoking we could hardly understand what he said. Notwithstanding as soon as he know that we were Spanish officers shook our hands and offered us something to drink. He asked us many questions about the French army, and it was then when he said a great sentence in very bad French: he was speaking of the defection of Bonaparte's allies and said very slow: *ceux qui ont tourné casaque avant Leipzig, bon camarade! Ceux qui l'ont tourné après, nix!* [Those who changed sides before Leipzig, good comrade! Those who changed after, nothing!][5] Before we took leave of him he desired the Mayor to lodge us all together in a good inn till the next day when his Colonel was to arrive and would provide for our *returning* to our country.

We could but admire the sudden changes of human life: the day before the smallest peasant of the village would have insulted us, and now the Mayor himself looked for his servant, gave him very particular instructions for to lodge us properly and make us comfortable, and begged our pardon for not going himself, *being* very *busy* about the Austrian officer. As soon as were lodged the Austrian officer *paid* us a visit, in which he showed us the greatest cordiality. His kind reception as well as that of all the Allied officers we have met in our journey *proves* very well that our behavior in running away from the places where we were on parole was no against our honour, for many circumstances had already disengaged us from this parole.[6]

These circumstances are worth to be known. First of all, the French government had so often cheated us, that we were, I imagine, in the right of cheating him once. Secondly the word we had given was not valid because we didn't enjoy the advantages of it: for we could not walk more than a mile from our depot and sometimes not that; and we were obliged to go every day to the *appel* [roll call] once; two or three times accordingly to the arbitrary will of our Commandant. Now every body knows that an officer who *promises* upon his honour to remain a *prisoner* ought to trusted, so then if he is as watched after this *promise* as before, it must be said that he is not under parole; and that the government who obliged him to make this *promise* only had the intention of having him in greater safety, but not to trust him, nor to give him any relief, consequently he is no longer enjoyned. But the greatest argument in our favour is the forgery committed in the act of taking our signatures by the *treacherous government* of Bonaparte, for in the beginning of our engagement where our names, rank, and qual-

5. The Battle of Leipzig in 1813 opened France to invasion by the allied armies.

6. See the discussion of the word of honor of captive officers in the introduction.

ities were written, they inscribed every one in a military degree lower than his own, in order to ascertain afterward that we had signed to be only of that rank. Many a one signed without reading. Some read it and asked to be qualified with their own ranks, but they answered them to sign it in that way if they did not like to be shut in a fortress. Others did not agree to sign it and were sent to the fortress in Flanders. The purpose on which this was done was still more horrid, for it was to avoid any further reclamation of our full pay, which they had already lessened to every one to a degree lower. After this it is impossible to find a single person who would think valid this kind of engagement where the French government was only endeavouring to cheat us. All this digression I deem it necessary to my friend to whom I like to show me as I am: full of honour, tho' I may have great many faults.

We were yet supping when a Spanish officer named Tolrá with his son 12 years old joined us. This man was a Catalonian of the lowest description yet, besides his rough manners, a very respectable man. He made his escape with his young boy in the same manner we did and this child followed him always walking. Although we did not *know* him, we admitted him in our company for being a Spaniard.

We supped very cheerfully and heartily and afterwards we went to bed, which we wanted very much. I must not forget that as we were lodged in the same inn where the soldiers were, they, during our supper, came one after the other to see us, and spoke us in their own language which we did not understand. They seemed very happy to see us for they all shaked hands with us and sang. We examined carefully their regimentals and arms, with what they were much pleased.

Here ends the 8th January. The 9th very early we were awoke by the landlady with the terribles: make haste the Austrians are going. We jump all out of our beds and half naked we run to the door. There I found all the detachment on horseback and the officer waiting for me to tell me that he was going forward to Chalon, and that we should stay for his regiment was to arrive there at 11 o'clock. But, replied I, we are not safe in this country as we have no arms. Never mind it, sayd he, they will not dare touch what is protected by the Allies; this looking over the peasants assembled round him. We then went to dress more quietly till the Colonel arrived. He told us that we were to go to the head-quarters of the advanced guard commanded by General Count Bubna, who would give us our passport.[7] On this purpose he ordered *carts* with oxen, the only to be found among those peasants, to convey us to Louhans, where an Austrian corps was to be that day, and from this to St. Amour where Count Bubna was. A Sergeant with a letter of introduction to the Austrian Commander at Louhans was also ordered, and before parting the Colonel's Adjutant who spoke very good French told us: *Messieurs, servez vous de l'autorité militaire lorsque vous serez a Louhans; ne prier pas beaucoup; commandez* [Gentlemen, make use of military authority when you are in Louhans; do not entreat much; command]. I shall never forget these words, for never in our lives we need more praying than we did at Louhans.

At three o'clock we set off upon four *carts* to each of them were two oxen, which went so slow as to want seven *hours* for nine miles. So we arrived at ten o'clock in the night at Louhans half frozen and torpid with the exceeding cold. Mr. Gros who could no more bear the cold sitting on the carts had gone before us walking near the Sergeant, and consequently arrived sooner at Louhans. What was his astonishment when upon asking for the Austrian Commander they answered him, that no Austrian had yet been seen in that country before that who was in his company. He immediately endeavoured to explain to the Sergeant what had happened, and make him quit directly that country, but it was needless, for the mob was already around him and would not leave him go, because they said he was a deserter. The Mayor and other magistrates came there and questioned him about his being there and about the number of troops remaining behind him. He said the truth of our case only he increased the number of troops and assured them that they were completely surrounded. They nevertheless insisted upon his remaining prisoner in that town, and the only thing they granted him was to go over where we were coming

7. Austrian field marshal, Count of Bubna-Littiz.

but in the company of a great number of citizens, while the Austrian Sergeant, who knew not a word of what was passing, was carried to the *Mansion*.[8]

During this we approached the town with the greatest confidence, but very soon the cries of Mr. Gros put us in a mournful consternation. *No Austrian is in this town!* said he, in the most desperate manner. These terrible news struck us in such a way that we could not profess a single word: only we jumped out of the carts and surrounded Mr. Gros in an agonizing silence. What can we do? was the first word professed after a great *pause*. Nothing, replied Mr. Gros; let us go to the Mayor's. *Blanco, no cree Vm. todavia esté libre?* [Blanco, do you believe that you are free yet?], said I, a reproach they made me very often since our depart, and followed Mr. Gros amidst the mob. In the mean time the Mayor called an Alsatian, named Paechler, who knew German, for questioning the Sergeant and to read the letter he had for the Commander of the Troops which ought to be in that town. This man was very usefull to us for as he know what a great care the Austrians took of us he said to the Mayor as it appeared afterwards that it was not prudent to stop us. We, by ourselves, made the same argument to the Mayor when we arrived to the Mansion. You know very well, said we to him, that the Austrians are at Tournus, St. Amour, St. Germain, and Chalon: if they are not come here today they will come tomorrow; what will then answer to them, when they will ask you, what the Spanish officers and the Sergeant are become? You must consider us now not like deserters, for being under the safeguard of our Allies we have recovered all the rights to our liberty. These reasons softened a little the Mayor, tho' he couldn't act openly as he liked on account of the mob: but without saying what he intended to do, he said; now, Gentlemen, I have prepared a very good inn where you can pass the night very comfortably and I promise you not to put you in gaol. Besides this we remarqued Mr. Gros speaking secretly with one

8. Fernando uses this term throughout the diary, presumably to mean the town hall (*mairie* in French).

of the Adjutants and having the appearance of being satisfied; with what a little hope began to rise in our hearts.

As soon as we were in the inn a guard of the citizens was established at the door, as well for to avoid our escape, as for prohibiting the mob to go in. The Sergeant did not know yet what was the matter of all those transactions, and was consequently as happy as possible for some Frenchmen and the Alsatian made him drink as much as he liked. We asked our supper to which we engaged the Sergeant, but then he was not so happy, for Mr. Gros, who had already won the confidence of the Alsatian, begged him secretly to explain all the case to the Sergeant. During the supper the same Adjutant came and spoke again with Mr. Gros: but it was only after supper when we knew positively that we could not nourish our hope of liberty, for Mr. Gros called me to the kitchen and told me that the Mayor wished us to return to St. Germain when the mob should be dissolved, but he asked a certificate signed by us all of his good behaviour with us for the sake of protection we had from the Austrians. I immediately wrote it and hurried every body to sign it.

All was done at two o'clock in the morning, we had also a guide to conduct us, and they were preparing the horse of the Sergeant. It was by the back door of the inn where we were to go out. I was one of the firsts with Mr. Gros; two or three more followed us, but we hardly had stepped out when we heard the sentinel crying. *Qui vit?* Of course we did not answer, but we ran as quick as we could. He then cried *La garde, le garde.* When we were at a distance we stopped to see if the others followed. Not at all, six were wanting, and the Sergeant. Very luckily we had the horse with us, and we took the resolution of waiting the others and in case that the people of Louhan should pursue us while we was waiting, Mr. Gros who was on horseback was to run immediately to St. Germain to ask assistance from the Austrians to deliver us. This was needless for soon after we saw all our friends coming. We hurried then the guide and walked as rapidly as it is impossible to imagine, tho' there was no road but only going through the mountains and the woods.

The 10th at five o'clock in the morning we were at St. Germain, and we must give great praise to the activity of Mr. Gros who by his restless care procured us the principal means of liberty in this terrible night. Before any thing we *called* on the Colonel to make him a sort of reproach for his having exposed our liberty, and ask him to be directed on the same way where we had come himself. He was quite surprised and vexed with this event, *but,* said he, *I am sure the Mayor would not dare stop you. Do not fear I shall abandon you no more. Go and take a little rest while the carts are prepared.* In a few hours all was ready for our departure, and as there are but carts drawn by oxen in that country, yet in order to make us go as quick as possible the Colonel ordered all the villages in the road to be waiting with their carts to supply one another successively. Notwithstanding these precautions, we went very slow, for, besides the natural slowness of the oxen, the roads in Bresse are horrid, that country being exceedingly marshy. The three days we had wandered in this miserable country were enough to make us long to see another. This we obtained the same day for we entered a very clean and healthy country, Franche-Comté.

In the first village we met a very unkind reception, for the Mayor would not give us more than one cart and this only because the Austrian Sergeant who came with us had no horse and did not like to walk; so we were obliged, tho' we had not any rest the night before to walk six miles more. My drowsiness was provoquing as I could not take three steps without falling asleep; which was dangerous too for the road was very slippery owing to the frost. Nor could the cold which was very great keep me from sleeping the whole way. At length we arrived at Lons-le-Saunier at eight o'clock at night. Then the Austrian Sergeant carried us to his Major's house who desired us to set off immediately to St. Amour if we wanted to see the general, but upon our observing that we were dead tired he gave us a note for the Mayor to secure us lodgings and carts for going the next morning at four o'clock to meet the general. We then first had the gratification of knowing that we were to be fed wherever we might be lodged. How gratifying this was can only be imagined by knowing that we had already spent almost all our money and had no means of subsistence but begging. The first instance of this new manner of life was very favourable and I was lodged in a Notary's house, a man of education and hospitality. I would enjoy but for a very few hours the comforts of the bed being obliged to go for the carts at four in the morning. But this was needless because the Mayor had kept the Major's order for the carts and now, had the impudence to deny that he had received such an order. Very angry with this we went and awoke the Major to ask him for another order, but he told us to go to the Place Comandant Captain Sebon an Austrian, who would oblige the Mayor to execute his orders.

Captain Sebon proved to be a very surly young man, aiming only to please the French magistrates in the town, perhaps to be rewarded by them. So that he approved of the Mayor's behaviour, and had the insolence to say to us that no prisoner was allowed to be conveyed by carts, and that he had gone as a prisoner from France to his country always on foot. I could not help telling him that I could walk as well as he could, and as for being a prisoner I thought I was no more so when I was among the Allies of my country. As things pressed it was very soon decided to go to St. Amour on foot, and in order to overtake Count Bubna in that place it was also decided that those who were less fatigued should walk on. I was among the number. I walked with all my strength till halfway where finding a public house I could not forbear proposing to my three companions to take a little rest and some breakfast. Before we had done the remainder of our party arrived at the same Inn and laughed at the great haste we made. They found that we could not be of much use in the affair and so it was found necessary to seek other means of overtaking the General. These were to send two of us in a post-chaise to St. Amour and if the General was gone to follow him while the rest should wait at St. Amour for them. Mr. Peter Porres and Mr. Miranda were chosen because they were so much fatigued that they could walk no more. The little Tolrá went also surely to avoid the fatigue of walking. The rest crawled on with the greatest pain. Our strength was quite exhausted and consequently our spirits were low. Notwithstanding to hear we were 4 miles from St. Amour I was seized by the whim to sing, endeavouring by that means to divest the cruel pains I suffered in my legs. Never was my throat so softened. This delighted me much, as singing is the thing in the world I should most like, and my companions were also pleased, and encouraged me to continue. I did so with pleasure when in the most pathetic part of a French song we heard the shot of a cannon. We all started at once and listened with eagerness to ascertain if we were not deceived, but the commotion of the firing removed all doubt. Everyone forgot his pains and my music, and only talked of the incident. This fear must not be attributed to cowardice, for without speaking of myself, there were among us some who had in Spain sufficient instances of gallantry; our fear was occasioned by the following considerations: we believed that we had nothing but Austrian cavalry before us, consequently the artillery we heard must be French, and of course the Austrian cavalry was to be driven away, and as we should not be able to follow them we certainly should fall into the hands of our enemies. The more we advanced the more distinctly we heard the firing and the more our terror increased, till upon our arrival at St. Amour we learnt that the Austrians were in great numbers near Bourg.

St. Amour at which we arrived the [11th], is a very small town, yet there are many families in it, in whose houses we were lodged and fed. One of them was called Mr. Lacroix, a surgeon. He was employed in an hospital to which many houses in my town of Seville belong. As soon as he knew the place of my birth he asked me to help him, when I should return to my country, to get the leases of them, which he has not been able to obtain since the beginning of the revolution. When in the morning arrived our two companions with the passport they had obtained from Count Bubna, to go to Basel where Count Schwarzenberg was to give us our further destination. By means of our passport and the activity of Mr. Gros we procured carts to turn back to Lons-le-Saunier. Our selfishness then betrayed itself manifestly for without any regard for those who went for the passport while we were sleeping, we took the best carts and left them the worst. The rain and the cold wind of the Mount Jura tormented us during the whole way, and we arrived at Lons-le-Saunier thoroughly wet. Captain Sebon with whom we were obliged to deal again for lodgings and carts, would not give us more than one cart, for, said he, the passport did not signify any more.

Notwithstanding, if the *Adjoint au Mairie*, who was there, could give us any more he knew he would do it, because he know him to be a very obliging gentleman. I could not believe what he said but as I could not understand the passport I was obliged to await the results of the good will of the *Adjoint* [Adjutant] the next day, and go for the present to the Mayor's to seek our billets. I happened to be lodged in the same house where I had been already tho' not in the same family. My landlord was a young married man who had been in Bonaparte's service against the Prussians and taken a prisoner, consequently he could not bear anybody who spoke German. Nor could he endure to see his country occupied by those who he himself had beaten many times. Yet he was reasonable enough to acknowledge that the Allies behaved better in France than the French did in other countries, and not only excused them for the requisitions they made in France but was very much pleased with it: for, said he, by that means France will know what a burthen it is to have the enemy at home and will rise against him and surely will drive him away. I could not dislike the boldness of this old soldier and his attachment to his own country, which did not prevent him from behaving very well to me.

Next morning very early I went in search of the carts for our party, I had then an opportunity of inspecting that little town, for I was obliged to walk all over it before I could find the gentleman to whom I spoke the day before at Captain Sebon's. This is the Capital of the Department of Jura; is rather pretty and clean; its principal wealth consists in a very large salt-manufactory. The building appeared very nice but I had not time to inspect it. I have been told by the natives that the process for the preservation of the salt is extremely curious.

The French gentleman was not at home and a very young boy, his only servant, let me in. He told me his Master was gone to mass and begged me to walk into the kitchen by the fire-side. No sooner was I seated then the little boy looking at my dirty shoes told me he was going to clean them, and I could not prevent him from doing it with the greatest eagerness. I was quite pleased with the kindness of this poor creature who by my appearance could not expect any reward from me. Soon after his Master came and made no objection to giving me four carts while Captain Sebon had said the day before that it was impossible to give us more than one. My companions were waiting for me in the Mansion already upon the carts without knowing they owed them to my activity. So that I very easily stopped their reproaches scolding for my long delay. We set off immediately and began to ascend the Jura mountains which are the vestibule to the Alps. These mountains are very ill-looking as they are nothing but stone and brush wood, notwithstanding the country produces a great quantity of excellent cheese of the same quality as what is called *Gruere* [Gruyère]. *A moitié chemin*[9] we stopped at an inn by the road side in which we partook of a luncheon of this cheese and some very bad wine in bottles twice as big as usual ones, the only kind they have in public houses in Franche-Comté. At the same time arrived there a young Valencian named Brotons, one of the worst characters among all the Spanish prisoners.[10] His company was one of the greatest evils which could have happened to us, for we not only had to endure the disagreeableness of an intercourse with such a fellow, but we were also exposed to give unfavourable impressions of ourselves to those who saw us in the company of a man who might behave as ill during the journey as he had done during his Captivity; yet as he was a Spaniard we did not dare to refuse him to be of our party.

After our luncheon we got again into our carts and followed our journey to Champagnoles where we arrived about twilight, very mis-

9. "half-way on" written above.

10. Francisco Brotons, a Valencian, was captured when the French laid siege to the city between November 1811 and January 1812. (It was also where José Porres was captured.) After the war, he was an ardent supporter of constitutional government and a prominent novelist. The cause of Fernando's dislike of him is unclear. They would re-encounter one another later in the trek across Europe.

erable indeed for the cold was very severe. This village is but a single street very long indeed and very broad. It is situated at the foot of a great mountain in a little valley very rich in iron mines which gave employment to the whole village. I with my constant companion Manuel Porres were lodged in a public house in which Count Bubna had been lodged for only one night, in which time his two Cossacks and two women had drunk nine bottles of the strongest brandy. The landlord received us very unkindly as is always the case with these people when they are not to be paid. Near the fire we saw two Hussars who appeared to be French. After enquiring what country they belonged to, they answered me they were French prisoners, taken by the Allies near Bourg and as they belonged to the countries over the Rhine the Allies sent them to their homes; but we very soon discovered they were deserters from the French army. One was a sergeant and two others soldiers. They had been a long time in Spain and one of them spoke very good Spanish. Their pockets were filled with Spanish gold and silver and the Sergeant had a very rich watch; the whole was but the fruit of their robberies in Spain. We supped together without ceremony during which time we had many arguments about Spanish and French troops. In one thing only they agreed, in their fondness for the Spanish girls. I availed myself of their knowledge of German to hear our passport read and then I learned the most essential of expressed in the words: *vagen und tappen fur flägön,* which I taught my companions and repeated very often for fun.[11] The meaning of them is that in every town they were obliged to furnish us means of conveyance and the necessary food. When we went to bed I was quite sorry to see we were to sleep in the same room with those robbers, for I expected to be robbed by them. My sleep was consequently very uncomfortable. Yet my fears were vain.

Next morning as they were going our way they joined us, so that our party was now increased by four people. The Sergeant had his own

11. Blanco White Family Collection, Manuscripts Division, Department of Rare Books and Special Collections, Princeton University Library, box 14, file 3.

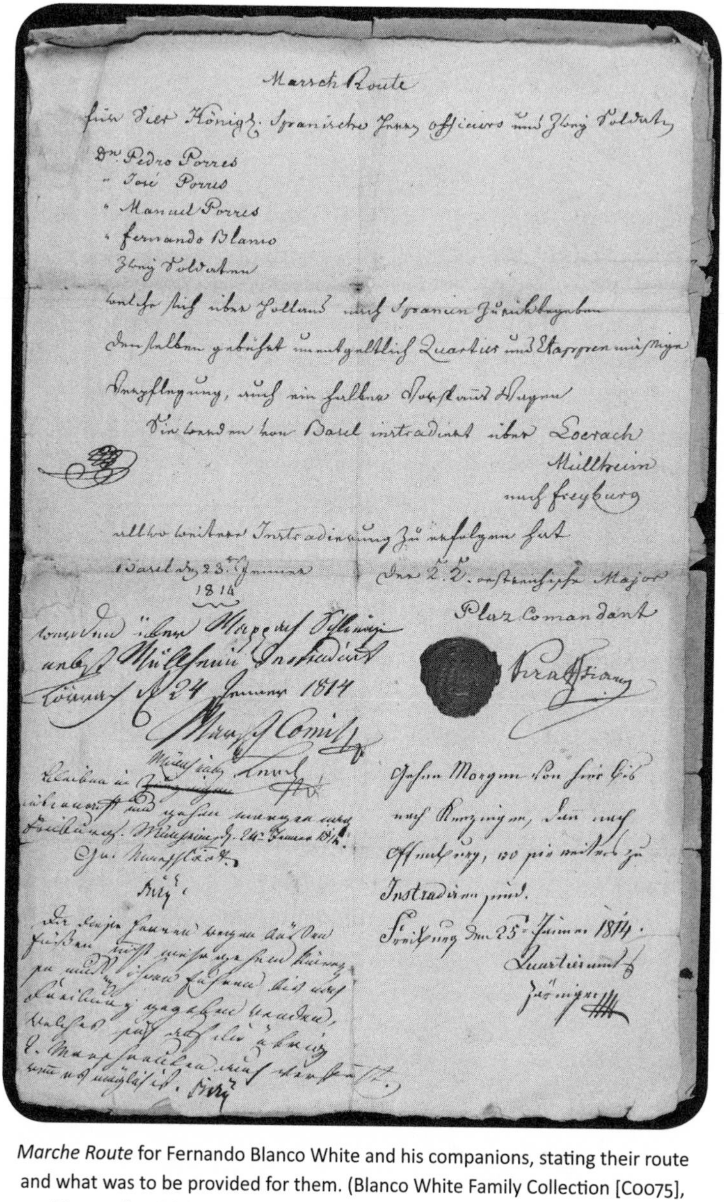

Marsch Route

Dn Pedro Porres
" José Porres
" Manuel Porres
" fernando Blanco

Loerach
Müllheim
nach Freyburg

Basel den 23. Januar
1814

Plaz Comandant

Müllheim den 24 Januar 1814

Freyburg den 25. Januar 1814.

Marche Route for Fernando Blanco White and his companions, stating their route and what was to be provided for them. (Blanco White Family Collection [C0075], Manuscripts Division, Department of Rare Books and Special Collections, Princeton University Library) horse, and the soldiers were invited to go in our carts, for which they were extremely grateful. Thus we began the journey of this day which was near 40 miles up very high mountains covered with fir woods. This kind of wood begins to be common in this country and continues the same in all Switzerland and part of Germany, being quite unknown in the center of France. The road we travelled now must be delightful in summer but at this time it was dreadful on account of the immense quantity of snow and ice with which it was covered. It was so cold that I could not remain in the cart and was obliged to walk up the mountains. When at the top of them I went into a public house to wait for the rest of my companions and warm myself. Very soon after one of them mounted on the Sergeant's horse told me that this fellow endeavoured by all means to become acquainted with them, and for that purpose had left him his horse to supply him in the cart among the others.

We had yet many miles to go on before we arrived at the place where we were to dine. This was a hamlet in which on our arrival we heard a peasant say to another *Chico, estos son españoles!* [Hey man, those are Spaniards!]. Anybody may imagine our astonishment at hearing a French peasant speaking as good Spanish as ourselves. We addrest them in the same language and inquired who they were, to which they answered they belonged to a depot of Spanish soldiers, and that they had obtained two years ago the liberty of earning their bread working among the French peasants.[12] It is impossible to conceive the transports of these poor wretches when they learned that we were Spanish officers returning home and that they might follow us if they wished. They did not dare leave us a moment not even to call their companions. One of these two was of the same Regiment of Mr. Brotons so

12. Jean René Aymes notes that the French government almost immediately mobilized the large Spanish captive population to work in various branches of the economy and as auxiliaries to the army and continued to do so right through 1813. Aymes, *Los españoles en Francia, 1808–1814: La deportación bajo el Primer Imperio* (Madrid: Siglo XXI, 1987), 169–74.

View of the Fort of Joux in Franche Comté, on the Frontiers of France & Switzerland, 1809 engraving. The fortress, near Pontarlier, had been taken by Austrian troops when Fernando Blanco White was passing through the area. (British Museum)

that from this moment he applied to him as his servant: the other went while we were dining to call the other Spaniards in the neighbourhood. Some of them did not choose to come. Four more came directly with great eagerness. Thus our party was increased by six soldiers.

During this the French Sergeant who had met in the road with a very pretty girl, one of those who follow the armies, was treating her splendidly without spending a farthing by an artifice of an old soldier. He went to an Inn speaking German and making a great deal of noise. The innkeeper believed him to be an Austrian and was so frightened that he gave him all he asked without paying as is the usual manner of conquering troops in the vanquished country. After his dinner he came to our inn; but here he had no need of deception, for Spaniards are extremely generous with women, and as they saw the girl there was nothing in the house which they did not offer her. She did not speak a word of French nor Spanish yet all my companions spoke to her, and she spoke to everyone. Cheerfulness reigned over the whole party, by the help of Bacchus and Venus. As for me, I was only indebted to the first, for I was still a philosopher. The girl continued with us till night in one of the carts, and the cold very soon put an end to our mirth. It was impossible to stay upon the carts and the nights increased our sufferings. At last by ten o'clock in the night the foremost of our party arrived at Pontarlier, for part of our companions remained behind in a village waiting for carts more than half an hour. This town was overrun with Austrian troops as it is very near the fortress of Joux, which had capitulated that day, but not yet surrendered.[13] This circumstance made the troops very vigilant, and consequently we were obliged to undergo all the formalities of entering a *place d'armes* which kept us very long before we were lodged. Tho' the town was crowded with troops the Mayor gave us very good lodgings. I went to the house of an old Demoiselle with Messers. Porres. A very good supper was waiting for us.

Near the table were two fellows who we should certainly have taken for banditti anywhere else. One of them was a German serving as a soldier in the English army who had been taken by the French in Spain and kept in prison for having attempted to escape, from which he had been lately delivered by the Austrians. The other was a Spanish officer named Alonso Bravo whose history is full of wonders.[14] As soon as he was taken prisoner four years ago, he ran away from his depot, and when in the frontiers of Spain was detected by a *Catalonian* woman and carried to France to a fortress;[15] but in his way he

13. Where Toussaint Louverture, leader of the Haitian Revolution, died in 1803.

14. A marginal comment says, "*Este Bravo era paysano y amigo intimo de Tomás González de Ximena*" (This Bravo was the compatriot and intimate friend of Tomás González de Ximena).

15. A marginal comment exclaims, "*mantilla en cima del gorro Adios!*" (mantilla on top of the cap, Adios!), perhaps meaning that under the traditional Spanish garb, the mantilla, the woman who turned him in was imbued with the revolutionary spirit symbolized by the cap.

deserted again, and again he was stopped after having received a shot in his shoulder. He was then sent to the very same fortress which he now saw in the power of the Allies, and he had the pleasure of seeing him who had kept him prisoner now a prisoner himself. From this fortress he escaped again with two more, one of whom was eaten by the wolves in the mountains. Soon after he was caught and while he was in gaol at Dole he learned the entrance of the Allies in France and their approach to that town. He then feared to be removed from that place where his deliverers were expected every day, and as he knew that only a real sickness could prevent the Gendarmes to remove him at the approaching of the Allies, he took the resolution of starving himself till it should be impossible to remove him. He succeeded perfectly, for when the French troops retired and took with them all the prisoners, they were obliged to leave him as he was near death. Very soon after the Austrian troops entering the town restored him to life and liberty. This hero of freedom had the greatest simplicity of manners, and sweetness of temper with his friends in which number we very soon were admitted.

In order to take some rest and wash our linen we asked the Austrian Commander the permission to remain one day in that town, which he granted very kindly; adding to this favor that of lending us some money of his own. The sum was about ninety francs which was divided among our party and another party of Spanish officers which had arrived the same day in the town. The Commander spoke with us a long time in French, which language he knew perfectly well. He told us that Joux would never have been taken by him if the garrison had had provisions, for its position rendered it impregnable even to those who might have guns of *gros calibre*, which he had not. He observed how providentially this fortress had been taken, for its guns were going to be employed against Besançon, which the Austrians had not yet attacked vigourously for want of guns *de gros calibre*. He took this opportunity to show us a very fine collection of maps of all the fortresses in France.

The remainder of the day we spent in visiting one another, and walking about the city. The principal part of which consists in a long and broad street with a gate at each end of it. The prospect on the Swiss side is closed by a high mountain upon which Joux is situated. Next day we set off early in the morning across a valley between two very high mountains covered with fir trees, called *le Val de Travers*. The whole road is but one street, for the villages extend themselves only in the direction of the road. The cleanness and industry of that blessed Switzerland began to appear and I gazed with enthusiasm at those small wooden houses, where nothing is wanting, in spite of the poverty of the country. The language in this part and in the east of the Principality of Neuchâtel is French, yet you can easily perceive that you are not in France. Our drivers missed the way, and instead of carrying us by the road of La Previene, they carried us all along the Val de Travers to the village of this name. At half way, the carts were to be changed, for which purpose we applied to the Mayor of a little village called [blank]. He was an ancient officer of the militia of the country, in the times when it belonged to the great Frederic.[16] His wife and his two charming daughters and the whole house were an instance of the greatest cleanness of Switzerland. All the family were extremely gratified to see officers of that nation which as they said gave the first example of resisting Bonaparte. The Minister of the Church was called to see us, and they seemed very serious of keeping us to dinner, but as we had yet about 12 miles to go further we could not stay any longer. Here for the first time I was driven in a *traîneau* [sleigh] the swiftest way of travelling that can be imagined. Near sun set we arrived at Val-de-Travers, where the Mayor received us with the greatest kindness. The best houses in the village were destined for our lodgings. I went with the Porres to a house where we had but one room for all four. Everything in it was wooden except the oven which was as all those of that country and great part of Germany of *fayence* [faïence] and they are kindled at the back of the room in order to prevent a current

16. Frederick the Great, king of Prussia (reigned 1740–86). Neuchâtel was returned to Prussian control after the defeat of Napoleon.

of air from being in the room as is the case with common ovens and chimneys, and which of course introduce the cold air in the room. I could not conceive at first this theory, but experience explained it, and I saw the reason why with so little wood the rooms were so warm.

The subsistence of the whole population in this Canton chiefly depends on the manufacturing of lace and watches. It is surely a singular contrast that of seeing the rudest people in the wildest country making the most delicate things which the hand of man can work.

The 17th in the morning we set off for *Neuchâtel*. The snow was very deep in the road, being over the highest mountains in the country. The horses could hardly draw the carts. When we were on the summit we were repaid for the badness of the road, by the enjoyment of one of the finest prospects I have seen in Switzerland, that of the town of Neuchâtel, the plain and the lake adjoining to it. This plain is bordered in the side of the town by a ridge of mountains which shelters the vineyards from the cold winds, and produces a very fine wine. I could hardly conceive how in those regions such good wine could grow.

Neuchâtel is in the bottom of the hill, which is so steep at its entrance that it seems as if you were falling into a precipice. We applied to a gentleman in the street to inquire for the Mayor, but he no sooner knew we were Spaniards, that he answered he was going to conduct us there. He carried us to the mansion, a most magnificent building, made at the expense of a private gentleman of that town who having acquired abroad immense riches, and dying without heirs, left it all for that purpose and building an hospital in the same town. We there met a great number of gentlemen who shewed us the greatest cordiality. They were there only for the purpose of having some of us in their own houses: and solicited this charge as a particular favour. Mr. Bravo fell to the lot of one of them who could speak nothing but Spanish, which the gentleman regretted very much, so that he begged me to leave him my companion Mr. Man.l Porres who spoke very good French, and take with me Mr. Bravo. Upon this we agreed immediately and consequently Mr. Bravo and myself went together to the house of a Minister called Meuron, which I had chosen as I always liked clergymen.[17] My choice could not be better for Meuron and his wife were the sweetest creatures in the world and the most beneficent, as they proved to Mr. Bravo to whom, with great delicacy, they gave many things he wanted in his dress. This respectable clergyman will be always dear to me as he was the medium through which the first tidings of my liberty came to England.

I won't attempt describing all his goodness to us both, nor the pleasure he took in listening to Mr. Bravo, who with the true national Spanish manner said in his own language to Mr. Meuron many things that I could hardly interpret. In the evening we were introduced to the Society of all the gentlemen of the town, no ladies being there admitted. A whole house is destined to this purpose. A large room for reading the newspapers and for conversation. Another for playing billiards, and another for smoking. The remainder of our party were also introduced by their hosts. The whole society had no other employment than that of entertaining us to their utmost. I was quite in an extasy, as any man must be, when after many years of oppression and dejection meets first with such marks of esteem. Their enthusiasm for what the Spanish nation had done extended to every individual, and looked upon every Spaniard as a hero of patriotism. In the effusion of my heart I could not help saying to them, that I wanted only one thing to make me happy in their company, that was to see them change their own language, for when I heard them speaking the language of my oppressors, I could hardly believe that I was among my best friends. *Ne craignez rien;* answered they, *notre langue est française, mais notre couer est bien loin de l'etre.* [Fear not. Our language is French, but our heart is far from being so.] It was quite true, for tho' they acknowledged that their former master Berthier had treated them very mildly,[18] yet

17. This is one of several joking asides to his brother Joseph, who was a priest and canon of the Seville cathedral's royal chapel before he abandoned Spain in 1810. In England, Joseph became an Anglican minister. Joseph would later send his son Ferdinand to study in Neuchâtel. Perhaps Meuron's letter was the origin of the connection.

18. One of Napoleon's marshals and his chief of staff, Alexandre Berthier, who governed as the Prince of Neuchâtel.

they could not bear the French government and rejoiced very much at coming again under the power of Prussia, as they were before the revolution of France. All the sacrifices they had made for the passage of the Allies by their Canton, they looked upon with satisfaction as they were intended to deliver them from the French yoke.

They gave me all the intelligence I asked about their country. I think they told me their population was one hundred thousand, and that they paid only one hundred thousand francs a year to Berthier, which is a trifling. They have a particular manner of insurance for their houses against fire. The whole Canton answers to every individual for his own house if it casually burns, and give him money to rebuild it.

Our way was traced out round the lake, which made it very long but these gentlemen went themselves to the Austrian Commander, to point out to him a shorter way for us, which was crossing the lakes of Neuchâtel and Morat [Murten] in a boat, and obtained from him the order to get a boat. We left the Society for supper, but with a promise to meet again in the morning, at the place of embarquement.

The place where we were to assemble was the mansion, and while I was waiting for our boat, I saw a Spanish soldier coming to us quite out of breath, and the first thing he did was to reproach the other soldiers, who were with us. This poor fellow was in the neighbourhood of the farm where we took the others, but they forgot to call him. When next day he knew that the others had gone, he took the resolution of following them, and walked by himself, procuring at every place intelligence about our way. He had walked incessantly till that very moment, when we were going on board. The boat was a small and open one, as are all that sail on the lake, but in order to make us a little warmer, the gentlemen of the town had ordered a great quantity of straw to be put in. We sat upon it, as close as possible for the boat was crowded, and after having bid adieu to our hospitable friends, we sailed to Morat [Murten] the 18th in the morning.

I could not have imagined that such a small piece of water could be so stormy; so that I was completely surprised, when upon leaving the shore, we began to be tossed about, as much as if we were on the sea. The rain, the snow and the rough wind increased the torments of the sickness, with which more than half the party were attacked. At last we arrived at the junction of the two lakes [Lac de] Neuchâtel and Murtensee; but here the wind was so contrary, that only to pass the short channel of junction, we were more than an hour. At the end of it is an inn, which we entered to warm ourselves a little. The innkeeper joined the sailors in begging us to perform the rest our journey by land, for it was impossible to them to cross the lake. All the sick were very much pleased with the proposal, and followed the master of the boat, who shewed us the way himself, though the others would rather have gone by the boat.

We walked by the side of the lake, which is exactly round, and in less than an hour we were at Murten, a small anciently fortified town upon a hill facing the lake. On the two sides of the only large street are spacious porticoes, in which all the shops are situated. This is the first town in our travels where we began to perceive the inconvenience of not understanding the Language nor the money. They speak very bad German, and they count by *batzen* [a local currency] a coin of the value nearly three *sols* of France. A great many people in the Mansion spoke French, as is the case in almost all the towns of Switzerland, so we were able to explain what we wanted. All was granted very kindly. A young gentleman carried me to his house, where he lived with his mother, a very good natured woman as well as I could perceive by her actions, for she could speak nothing but German. She gave me a provisional dinner, at which I first ate a kind of soup peculiar to the country: its broth is black and as thick as pap. I remembered the favourite dish of the Lacedaemonians [Spartans].

After dinner I went to the Minister's, where Mr. M. Porres was lodged, and when I met a Surgeon who spoke very good Spanish having been in Spain a long while in the French service. It is to him that I am indebted for the intelligence about the best German grammar, Meidinger's. My landlord had promised me to introduce me to the Society of the gentlemen, but he had gone to a kind of alehouse with a newly arrived friend of his. His mother took me there, and I met him with two more eating herrings and drinking wine. They obliged me to take a share of their repast, which lasted for three hours, without any variation in their dish. During the whole time they were smoking. After this we went home to take our supper. This young gentleman loved the French very much, among whom he had long lived. He said that it would have been a very easy thing for Switzerland to prevent the Allies crossing their Territory. He could not bear the coldness of the Austrians, of which he gave an instance in an Officer, who after having been in his house, and treated with every kind of attention, uttered the only word *Adieu* upon his taking leave. I was quite surprised at this for, I as yet knew not their relations in coldness, the English.

Next morning before I left him, he shewed me the *Lausanne Gazette*, which the numbers of Spanish officers who were crossing Switzerland were mentioned, in their return home.[19] After breakfast we got into the carts that were provided for the first part of that day's journey; during which time I endeavoured to learn the most essential things in the German language, for my own use. In this work I was helped by the driver of my cart, who was a young fellow of the greatest simplicity, as will appear by this single instance: he told me he was extremely pleased to convey people that were not Russians and upon my asking, how could he know that we were not Russians? he answered me; *Ah, j'ai un [su?] desuite que vous etes moins grossiers qu'eux* [I knew right away that you are less coarse than they are]; a very nice compliment indeed, which made us laugh very cordially. We crossed a great many streams, some of them very large; they must embellish in summer that beautiful country. At the time I saw them their appearance was not gratifying, as it was very cold weather, but we had many other

19. The January 18, 1814, number of the *Gazette de Lausanne* reported, "*Nous avons vu arriver ici une cinquantaine d'espagnols, qui, prisonniers de guerre en France, ont trouvé le moyen de s'echapper et de joindre les alliés. Ils ont obtenu ici des feuilles de route pour l'Allemagne.*" (We have seen fifty Spaniards arrive here, who, prisoners of war in France, found the means by which to escape and to join the Allies. They have obtained here passes for Germany.)

things to please our eyes; the beauty of the prospects, the aspect of the houses, built in a particular shape, and above all the variety and oddity of dresses. It would be as difficult to remember them all, as to describe them: and if I had been a painter, surely I should have spent my time in taking sketches of them. I must not forget a singularity in this country, that all the bridges are covered with a straw roof, which gives them more the appearance of a farmhouse, than that of bridge.

When we arrived at the village, where the carts were to be changed we found ourselves for the first time in the predicament of not being at all understood. I began then to be the interpreter of our party, tho' I knew not more than five or six words of German. I showed my passport and cried very loud *trei sagen* [*sic*], which I repeated to every question the Mayor asked me. In about half an hour all was ready, for the continuation of our journey to Berne, and the nearer we approached it the more the country became beautiful. Its environs are covered with an immense number of gentlemen's country houses. As the country is a vast plain, spotted with little hills, nothing could be better for that purpose; for all these houses are situated each on the top of a hill. The town itself is extremely nice. A great number of very handsome buildings embellish it, but what renders it nice beyond expression is the continued portico on each side of the streets by which you are sheltered from the inconveniences of the weather; and the small stream of the purest water running perpetually in the center of the street, by which means all kinds of dirt is carried away in a moment. If I am to judge by the number of shops this town must carry on a considerable traffic; yet by the fine appearance of the upper parts of the houses it may be judged that they do not belong to the shop-keepers, but to people of quality, to which I am very much inclined for I believe that the meeting of the Diet takes place in this town. My reason for thinking so is that this town was the residence of two Ambassadors, that I knew those of Spain and Italy. The first called Lieut. General C[a]amaño was an old Gallician, extremely attached to his country; and abhorring whatever belonged to the invader Joseph Nap.[20] He had refused to represent him and consequently during the occupation of Spain by the French, he had not received his pay and was in great misery. He had many friends in Switzerland who wished to supply him with money, but he never accepted it. As he was poor we did not go to see him. I am the more ashamed of this as afterwards, while we were at Freybourg [Freiburg], this poor man was very useful to us.

I knew of the Italian ambassador, because I happened to be lodged in the house, where he lived. It is a custom in that town, in houses where several families live, to give the garret to some poor family with the burthen of lodging every military man, where the Mayor may send to any of the tenants. I was sent to one of these houses, and tho' in the garret, I must own I was very comfortably off. My landlady was a tall thin old woman, speaking very little French, but there came a very nice boy, who spoke very well, and who had the whim of waiting on me at dinner. I say the whim for he was no less than the son of the Italian ambassador. I went out after dinner to buy the German grammar, and as soon as I came home the boy called on me with his tutor, an Italian priest, who addressed me in his own language. I answered him without hesitation in the same language tho' I don't know half so much of it as I do of English. Notwithstanding our conversation was very long, and ended with the offer of a bottle of good wine for my supper. I refused only from ceremony, but I was very happy to find that they did not mind my refusal. I was not so happy when I saw my landlady sitting down to supper with me and drinking very hastily the half of my beloved bottle. She was in such high spirits that I am very much afraid, had she not been so dirty, that we should have shared but one bed.

20. José Caamaño served for many years in Portugal and Switzerland. Though he might have told Fernando and his friends that he was opposed to the *rey intruso,* he had served Joseph I until the embassy to Switzerland was suppressed in 1811. In other words, he would come to be known as an *afrancesado* for having sworn loyalty to and served Joseph I.

The government at Berne do not allow *putas* [whores] to live by themselves: they are obliged to be under its immediate inspection in the *bagnois* [brothels]. One of my companions told me every particular relative to those houses. There are rooms of every description, according to the price. To judge by the costume, it may be said that the house is filled with women of every rank, from the country girl to the lady of fashion. But all is deceit for the Duchess this evening becomes a country girl the next morning. These wretches pay a great part of their gain to the house. I have been told that they all of them ring a bell when they are going to bed. But I don't know for what purpose, for nobody comes to their call. It is to be sure a horrid thing to think, that such places exist in the world, yet it must be owned that many evils are prevented by them. What distance, great God, between the riotous scenes in those places, and the sweet intercourse of two tender virtuous lovers! Yet the former is but the corruption of the latter. To what depravity will not man arrive!

The 20th in the morning I got up very early, I took my coffee with my landlady who was surprised to see how much bread I ate, comparatively to her, who ate but three or four ounces a day. After this I went all about the town, to try to assemble all my companions for as we did not agree the day before upon a meeting place, one went one way while others went another. At last with many pains we assembled in the place where the carts were to be delivered, but then we met with another delay, for the order didn't include as many carts as we wanted. I was obliged to run again to the Commissary's to get our due, which was not an easy thing to obtain.

On leaving the town towards Soleure [Solothurn in German] the ground descends at once considerably to a small river, and then rises again to a position very favorable for considering the aspect of Berne. It is astonishing how confused are my ideas of what passed this day. I can only ascribe it to my bodily indisposition of that day. I have a confused remembrance like that of a dream, that halfway on we entered an Inn by the road, where every one of us took something to eat, while I remained by the oven reading. Just as we were going out we met two Spanish Colonels, who had fled from their depot conducted by a Catalonian to whom they had paid a large sum of money to be carried down the Rhone to Spain; but as they reached Mâcon they met with the Allies; and thought it preferable to go through the Allied army, rather than continue their intended route. We pursued ours with great diligence till we were detained by an accident to one of our carts. Nobody was hurt and the cart required but little time upon it, so as to be able soon to follow the others.

We very soon discovered the old ugly-looking Soleure. This town anciently fortified as are almost all those in Switzerland is situated upon uneven ground. A broad but shallow river runs through the lower part of it. A long wooden bridge joins the suburb to the town. Mr. Ml. Porres and I were lodged in the filthy house of a barber. The barber's father was a shoemaker, a very good natured man indeed, who endeavoured to make us as comfortable as their houses would allow of. There was a Clergyman who had been a Chaplain in a Swiss Regiment in Spain. His Regiment having been only in Catalonia he could speak no other dialect yet that was enough for us to understand each other. Sometimes he spoke Latin, sometime French but always with great volubility which he accompanied with gestures and movements enough to make anyone laugh who was not in such low spirits as myself. He told us of the magnificent cathedral in their town and awoke our curiosity to see it. To this we complied after dinner and it must be owned that it is one of the most beautiful I ever saw in the modern architecture, and certainly the best situated of all which I have seen; for it stands upon the highest ground in the town and facing to a long and broad street where the best houses are.

After we had satisfied our curiosity we intended to call on our friends, but as we did not know where they were lodged we began to inquire of those we met in the street. Nobody could understand us till at last a Gentleman, wrapped up in a cloak in the Spanish style, came to us inquiring very civilly what we wanted. He then ordered one of his men to gain intelligence about their lodgings, and in the meantime he told us that all his family had served the king of Spain.

He himself had been in Wimpffen's Regiment, and had obtained from our king the order of Charles 3rd.[21] When his man came we took leave of him and went to our friends. All of them were lodged in a publick house kept by a man who had been a lieutenant in the Spanish army where he had remained for more than 15 years. He showed us his regimentals, his Spanish sword, his titles, and told us his whole story in Spanish, notwithstanding which he starved my poor companions. It is an observation, that will always hold good, that almost all those foreigners who, as we say, have eaten the Spanish bread, behave very ill to Spaniards when they get them in their country. I could never know the reason of this but experience has confirmed it in many instances.

In the same room where we were I noticed a man drinking a bottle of wine by himself, whom I very soon knew to be a freemason; he noticed me also and came immediately to me to offer me a friendly share of his bottle. I could not refuse. The man was so delighted that I began to be uneasy for my head, for in his ecstasy he made me drink bumper after bumper without respite. As soon as I could get rid of my freemason I went home to supper. There we sat at table with the shoemaker and his sons, their wives, journeymen and prentices. After supper they carried us to an inn dirtier than any I have ever seen in Spain. A nasty bed was prepared for Mr. Porres and myself. Had it not been so cold we would have sat up the whole night rather than have got into such a bed but the cold vanquished our repugnance.

We awoke very early in the morning, and went immediately to the shoemaker's to get our coffee, the ordinary breakfast throughout Switzerland. While we were breakfasting a man came from Mr. de Glutz Ruchty to ask us to breakfast with him. This was the gentleman we had met the day before, a man of quality who had been Landaman [chief magistrate] of Switzerland. All dirty and greasy as we were we entered a magnificent house where we met the gentleman who told us how sorry his wife had been that he had not kept us the day

21. Luis Wimpffen, a Swiss officer who served in the Spanish military from the 1790s to the 1820s.

before. She might have been very sorry for it, but I dare say she was not so much so as ourselves. The Lady herself repeated the same compliment to us, which increased our regrets. During breakfast he told me what had happened to their only son. This young man was a Captain in the Spanish service in Wimpffen's Regiment. He was taken prisoner by the French who promised him many advantages if he would join them. He had the imprudence to accept their offers without consulting his father, who did not approve of his resolution tho he was much pleased to have this opportunity of seeing him. He remained some time at his father's but no sooner had he joined his French regiment in Spain than he was taken prisoner by the English and brought to England to Bridgnorth in Shropshire. His father was endeavouring to exchange him at the time I was there, and as he knew that I was coming to England he gave me his son's direction that I might write to him upon my arrival and give him intelligence about his family. Very happily I believe my letter was of no use, for I was told in Germany that all prisoners belonging to the countries occupied by the Allies were coming home. Notwithstanding this I wrote him as soon as I arrived.

Before we took leave of his father he gave us a direction where we might have our dinner half way on the road to Ballenbourg [Waldenburg]. We accepted of this kindness owing to our absolute want of money, tho' in other circumstances our pride would never have permitted it. Our companions had already mounted the carts storming at us for the delay we occasioned. We set off and pursued our journey, which was rendered very uncomfortable on account of the occasional thaw. The aspect of this country is extremely whimsical; it is almost as if they had put a great number of detached rocks upon flat ground leaving narrow alleys between them. The place where our carts were to be changed was commanded by a young Swiss officer who lived in a very nice house, and who kept, I do not know for what purpose, the names of all the Spanish officers who passed by that place. The number was already very considerable. While the carts were preparing Mr. M. Porres and myself went to the house to which we were directed from Soleure. It was an Inn, the master of which was the uncivilest of creatures. Nevertheless he gave us a good dinner but as I was afraid that he might ask Mr. de Glutz more than his due I proposed to him to give a receipt for what we had had against that gentleman. He was much pleased with my proposal, so I gave him a receipt for the immense sum of 24 *batzen*.

By this time the carts were ready to continue our journey. This country was quite different from the other. This was very mountainous and woody. The thaw had not reached it; on the contrary, it was extremely cold so that I preferred walking to going by the carts. I went the whole way on foot, which tired me very much by the time I had arrived at Waldenburg. We called on the Commissary for our lodgings, but what was our astonishment when he answered us very rudely that he could not give us any lodgings first because the village was full of sick from the army and secondly because his village was not one of those destined to lodge military men. We did not mind what he said, but only shewed him our passport, where the name of that place was marked for our station, and cried aloud the single word *quartier, quartier.* He put himself in a passion, and believing perhaps that we should respect him more he put on in a great hurry his military coat and his sword. We could not help laughing at his simplicity, and in spite of his regimentals we continued to ask for our lodgings. In this manner we remained more than an hour, till at last we saw that it was impossible to obtain anything not even carts to pursue our journey. We then asked if there was not some magistrate in the village above the Commissary, to which we were answered in the affirmative. The Commissary himself sent a man with me to that Magistrate who said very civilly that it was not in their power to lodge us, but that they would endeavour to get us two carts to continue our journey to Liegstall [Liestal] three leagues further. I reported this answer to my companions who were not at all pleased as it was near night and very cold and they had taken no dinner, but there was no remedy.

Two carts could not take the whole party. The Commissary knew this well enough and for that reason he began to hurry our soldiers to set off on foot while the carts were preparing. I believe he was afraid of us and wished by all means to get rid of us. Not only the soldiers but a great many of our companions began to walk in the hope that we should very soon overtake them. I remained for the carts as I was tired. The carts were not ready for half an hour, so it was dark when we set off. Our drivers hurried as much as their horses would permit, yet we could not overtake those who went on foot till the two thirds of the way. The poor wretches were out of breath, as people who had not had any dinner. All of them took places in the carts.

We arrived very soon at Liestal, and we were happy enough to get lodgings immediately, but what lodgings gracious God! Messers Porres and myself were sent to a cutler's, who said he had learned his trade in England; he had not learned, as we could perceive, neither the cleanliness nor the wealth of the English, for he was very poor and his house very dirty. He asked us if we wished to have some pastry for our supper? We answered we wanted meat tho' we repented very soon, for he gave us a piece of boiled beef so hard, that it was impossible to eat it. As for beds he said he had none, but he had warmed one of his rooms, where we might lie upon clean straw and cover ourselves with some blankets he would spare of his own, and family. In short we might say that there was nothing in the house but our landlords' good will and kindness. In these he was not sparing, for he was the best man in the world, in so much that notwithstanding the bareness of his house we could not be angry. We only laughed at the magnificence of the common bed he was preparing for us all upon the floor. It was a different story with Mr. Martinez who entered the room at this moment with four more. He was astonished at seeing us there, and we were not a little surprised to see him come to our house. The case was that they were lodged in the house of our landlord's relations, who having not only no beds to give them but not even a warm room, had taken them to ours. They were not aware of this till they saw their landlord spreading straw in a corner. Mr. Martinez was so much disappointed that he flew into a passion, which increased our laughter. At last the fatigues of the day and the drowsiness overpowered our laughter and Mr. Martinez's passion. We slept very quietly though not very long, for before daybreak we were all in very merry conversation, even Mr. Bidza who owing to a pique against Mr. Martinez had lain upon the floor. Breakfast came afterwards to keep up our mirth, for it was of the same description as the supper. I then first tasted a kind of liquor distilled from plums, of a very bad flavour. Upon this occasion I was confirmed in my opinion that spirits are necessary to mankind, for it is impossible to conceive their ingenuity in extracting them from every thing.

After breakfast we got into our carts with directions to Basel, from which we were but 12 miles, and where we expected to find Count Schwarzenberg,[22] to whom we were directed by Count Bubna. In our way we saw for the first time the Rhine, though we could not believe it, for the erroneous idea we always form, that large rivers must be so, even in their source. On our arrival at Basel the 22nd of January we learned that the day before the Allied Sovereigns had left the town. Schwarzenberg was no longer there, and we knew not to whom to apply in his stead. At the Mansion they referred us to the Austrian General commanding in the town. He told us that there was a Spanish Ambassador there to whom we might apply yet we need not take that trouble for he could do nothing for us. After this he gave us the order for our lodgings, which we took to the Mansion; but here we were told that no lodgings for officers were remaining, and consequently we could only be lodged as soldiers. We took them as they were, but we could not remain in them, for it is impossible to conceive how filthy they were. The second lodgings I got for myself and Mr. Man.l Porres was for soldiers likewise, but the landlord the good Euler Schneider, that is, Euler tailor, when he saw that we were not soldiers cleared his shop to lodge us in it as comfortably as he could. He did everything

22. Prince Karl Philip Schwarzenberg, Austrian field marshal, who commanded forces in many of the major battles of the era both for and against Napoleon. He took part in the invasion of Russia in 1812 but then led the Austrian armies against his erstwhile ally at Dresden, Leipzig, and during the invasion of France.

so kindly that though we could not understand him we could see his good nature.

We got some dinner and called afterwards upon our companions. Mr. Peter Porres was of opinion that we ought to call on our Ambassador. I did not chuse it for I dislike extremely the coldness with which those who are employed by the Spanish government behave to their countrymen. I was obliged to vanquish my repugnance and follow Mr. Porres' advice, because his reasons convinced the others. No foreigner can travel without a passport from his country Magistrates or from some of the Ambassadors of his country. In consequence of this we called upon the Ambassador Dn. José Pizarro, the Minister of the King of Prussia.[23] We found him in a room filled with trunks, papers, beds, chairs all topsy-turvy. He was wrapped up in his *capa parda* smoking a cigar, surrounded by his secretary, his state messenger and some Spanish officers in the greatest familiarity. Mr. Porres asked him for a passport for all of us to return home by Trieste; but very fortunately he pointed out to us the inconvenience of both things; first if we were all included in the same passport we should be obliged to continue always together, and secondly if we went to Trieste we should with difficulty find means of embarking, as there is but little commerce between that place and Spain. The best way, said he is by Holland to England. Nothing can suit me better said I, for I have there some relations. The Secretary Mr. Onis noticed this answer, when I gave him my name to be inscribed in the same passport of Messers. Porres,

23. Pizarro had arrived a few days before, traveling with the king of Prussia. See his communication dated Basilea, 18 de Enero de 1814, Archivo Histórico Nacional (Madrid), Sección de Estado (hereafter AHN/E), legajo 5936, despacho 54. José García de Léon y Pizarro was practically born into the royal service—his father was a member of the Council of the Indies and captain general of Quito. Pizarro held diplomatic posts in Berlin and Vienna before 1808. During the War of Independence, he served as minister of state in Cádiz. He was named minister to the Prussian court in 1813. After the war, he held high offices under Ferdinand VII but eventually embraced the liberal cause and spent several years in exile. He wrote his *Memorias* of the era, which were published several decades after his death.

and asked me if by chance I was a relation of B. W. in London.[24] Yes indeed, answered I very earnestly, thinking I had already found one of his friends. Well, said Mr. Onis, as a friend I advise you, when you are in London not to see him, for his behaviour has alienated from him all true Spaniards.[25] That I will not do, replied I, for he is my brother. There the conversation ended on both sides, till Mr. Porres spoke to the Ambassador about our want of money. This complaint he answered by a similar one of his own, but that we might call next day to learn the results of a little negotiation he had begun with the English Ambassador to get some money to relieve the numbers of Spaniards that continually were applying to him.[26]

The night was now far advanced so we went home to get our supper and go to bed. The good Euler took us to his table among his nice children. One of them in his neat regimentals of the militia and the other in the modest dress of those who are preparing for holy orders. Both spoke French and were as good as their father. The former gave me all the intelligence I wanted about the fortress of Hunninghen near that town; the latter gave me some information in the German language and lent me some books for that purpose. Every one in the house was kind to us; for the landlady washed our linen and the journeymen mended our clothes without permitting us to pay. Is it possible that a poor wretch as I was, nearly a dependent should find so much goodness among people who were themselves in such a low station!

24. Mauricio de Onis. See AHN/E, legajo 5936, despacho 55, "Avisa la llegada a este Quartel general de D. Mauricio de Onis y de D. Justo de Machado, y el recibo de los oficios de 5, 6, y 11, de O.tbre y de 9 de Nov. re." Dated Basilea 18 de enero de 1814. El Ministro de S.M. cerca del Rei de Prusia [Pizarro].

25. On Joseph, see the introduction. His editorship of *El Español* in London incurred the wrath of the Cádiz government, expressed succinctly by Onis.

26. Pizarro reports on this negotiation with Aberdeen in "Avisa la llegada de varios oficiales Espanoles fugados de Francia, y repite la necesidad que hay de que se le autoriza para socorrer a los que vayan llegando," Basilea, 16 de Enero de 1814. AHN/E, legajo 5936, despacho 52.

You, poor Euler, and a few others will reconcile me with humankind, and prevent me from falling into misanthropy.

The next morning we waited upon the Austrian general to ask a passport, for as we were going to cross Germany we thought a German and military passport preferable to a Spanish one and not given by a military man; tho' we could keep this for other occasions. The general was a little angry with us for our intruding upon his time, as it appeared by his manner of answering. He sent us directly to the Mansion to get the passports. The whole morning was spent here to get them, and after all they were but Marche-Routes annexed to the Spanish passports. As we had very little expectations from Mr. Pizarro we asked for carts to continue our journey. Very luckily we could not get sufficient number for our party, by which means we had a share of the money he got that evening for the prisoners. I was very happy to learn that there was some money for us: I was still more so when we got twenty Frederics (about 20 guineas) to be discharged by our Regiments; but nothing can be compared to my happiness when upon descending the stairs I met with my dear son Flamis (Mr. Joseph Keyser) who had fled two days before myself.[27] I clung to his neck if not with the tenderness of a father at least with that of a very good friend. Mr. Cardenas too was with him and some others whom I knew but little. Their delay was owing to the turn they had made in their way passing by Geneva. Yet he was indebted to this delay not only for the pleasure of seeing me but for that of lodging in the house of General Tomini's [Jomini] Mother near Geneva. This officer was one of the most learned military men in Bonaparte's army: whom he deported after the affair at Dresden.[28] My son was to remain next day at Basel

27. Not literally his son. Perhaps some kind of bond formed under the conditions of captivity. Gil Novales's historical dictionary notes a "José Kaiser," who was the Secretario Politico de Huelva in 1823 (vol. 2, p. 1605).

28. Baron Antoine Henri Jomini, a Swiss officer who served Napoleon but went over to the allies toward the end of the wars.

and consequently we were obliged to part very soon. The town was so overburthened with the passing of troops that it was very difficult to find means of conveyance. The experience of those who were still waiting for carts after three or four days of expectation, taught us to mistrust every promise of carts, and to walk to the first village in Germany where we were quite sure of getting them.

The 24th by day-break we crossed the Rhine upon the wooden bridge at Basel, not so fine but as long as Westminster's. The town we left now behind us is a very large one, and must be very commercial, if we consider its situation in the confines of France, Germany and Switzerland; but it is very ugly and gloomy. I noticed in it a very odd custom; that of putting two or three looking-glasses on the outside of each window, in different directions that any thing passing in the streets might be seen in the room, without stirring. The morning was very cold and the snow very deep: if the former hastened our pace, the latter abated it. We arrived at the village where we expected to be relieved from our fatigues, but we were quite disappointed. Whether they had no carts, or what was more likely, they thought themselves under no obligation of obeying our passport since those who had given it had not executed their own orders, we were obliged to walk the whole day. At our repeated entreaties the Mayor wrote something in our passport and told us that by that order we should have carts in the next village, and dinner too. When we arrived at it, the Mayor's wife undeceived us about what was written in the passport. It was only said there that it had not been possible to give us carts. I was not surprised for I never believed what he told us; for even if he had written what he said, he had no authority over another Mayor, and consequently he would not have been obeyed. What surprised me most was to find that everybody refused to sell us anything to eat. We produced our money to prevent any doubt that might arise about us, but nothing would prevail upon them to sell us the smallest bit of bread; for when once Germans say *nix nix*, every effort to convince them is useless. We cursed these people with the utmost anger, and began to regret France, where nothing is refused for money, even in houses where no shop is kept.

Hungry and angry as we were we undertook our journey with the forlorn hopes of finding an Inn five mile farther. Very seldom have I been so hungry. I think I could have eaten in that moment bread rejected by the dogs, How charming was to me the appearance of the wished-for inn! Some boiled beef, *soucrout* [sauerkraut], and cheese made one of the most delicious dinners I have ever eaten. The wine too and the *Kirsch waser* added something to my happiness, in as much as making me forget all my fatigues. I must not forget the meaning of these two German words: *soucrout* is literally sour-cabbage and it is but shredded cabbage kept in brine till it comes to the state of fermentation, which gives it a very nice taste of acidity. They make great use of it in Switzerland and all Germany, only boiled with *porc*, which makes a very good dish. *Kirsch waser* or cherries-water is a kind of spiritous liquor extracted from cherries. There is some to be found very good, tho' generally it is too strong. This, I think, will be a proper place to notice that the Mayor is called in German *Burgmeister* [Bürgermeister] that is, town-master, which word the French have corrupted *Bourguemestre* by which title we always called the German mayors.

Before we left the inn the landlady came to me with a great air of mistery and said; I dare say you are to pass by Offenburg; then I take the liberty of advising you to shun the Post inn at that town for they are quite robbers. Here she began to inveigh against the innkeepers of the already mentioned inn and should have continued if I had not lost my patience in listening to her. Her husband came afterwards to me with the same story, from which I perceived that there was perhaps some enmity between those two innkeepers, and that consequently they endeavoured to mislead the customers from one another's houses.

We left his place in great good humour and walked very stoutly towards Milheim [Mülheim]. I was in such spirits that Mr. Gros and Mr. Martinez kept always by my side to enjoy my chatter. But the case was otherwise when we arrived about night at our destination, for my feet were so crippled that I could hardly stand upright. The Commissary of this small town wished to send us three mile further, and it was but to our repeated solicitations that we owed our remaining that night there. The Bürgermeister was more civil. We obtained from him very good lodgings. Mr. Man. Porres and myself were lodged in the house of one of the first gentlemen in the town, tho' not the first patriot, for as he was in his business extremely connected with France, he found fault with everything which the Allies did. Private matters augmented his hatred. His corn, hay, cattle, and everything in his house had been consumed by the perpetual passing of troops. Every piece of furniture that was portable had been stolen by the soldiers. In spite of this he behaved very civilly to us tho' it was very easy to see that this was nothing but politeness. He gave us two very nice beds. How much I enjoyed the pleasure of sleeping alone! I wish all my friends could know this enjoyment, for a bed to one's self after a long day's journey on foot is one of the greatest blessings in human life. While we were undressing we remembered the comical adventure we had witnessed at the Mansion: a Bavarian soldier quite drunk but very steady was speaking with great quickness and cheerfulness to everybody in his own language, which nobody understood. When he saw us he spoke to us with marks of a very distinguished friendship, particularly to Mr. Bravo, very possibly on account of his green coat, for this is the colour worn by their *troupes d'élite.* This preferment for Mr. Bravo was again manifested the next morning in the same place, for all the Russians came to him, and obliged him to eat and drink with them.

It was in vain that we waited for carts more than an hour. The Mayor told us it was impossible to get enough for all of us, but he would endeavour to give one for those who absolutely could not walk. Five or six of them remained to go in the cart, while I walked with the rest towards Freiburg. As soon as we began to proceed I noticed the singularity and beauty of the place we passed through which continued the same as far as Francfort [Frankfurt]. The Rhine flows directly from south to north with a ridge of mountains not very high at a distance of 6 or 8 miles from its right bank. This side of the mountains being sheltered from the easterly winds proves very good for the vine. So that they are covered up to their top with this useful plant. To conceive how well adapted the soil must be for the vine, it is enough to know that tho' the grapes in Burgundy had not come to complete maturity for the last three years, yet near the Rhine the wine of these three vintages was not sour; a proof that the grapes were ripe.

The space between these mountains and the Rhine is a beautiful plain rich in corn and fruit trees. The road is through this plain, at the foot of the mountains. It is always bordered by cherry trees, which must embellish it beyond every thing in summer. The road in itself is extremely fine. Rather broader than those in England and far better, at least as far as I saw. It was very cold but less so than the preceding day, which had been one of the most severe during the journey, for I never shall forget that in spite of my [blank][29] woolen jacket and waistcoat, and tho' I was loaded with my little knapsack, and walked very fast yet the cold was insupportable. Whereas I now found my knapsack and clothes too much for me one of the greatest proofs of not being very cold. This was one of the dullest days in our travels. Our weariness and the continual mortifications we experienced from the Austrians and Russians created us much vexation. They thought we were French, and consequently every one stared at us with looks expressive of their anger and contempt. We could not understand what they said, nor make them understand that we were not French; all we could do was to cry out to those who approached us too near *Nix frantzoose, Spani*: which words as they belong to no language were understood by every nation. I think nature taught us this language for our preservation.

About one o'clock we dined at an Inn by the roadside, but the wine could not even put us in spirits. My feet were very sore, and my spirits extremely low. I could not believe that we were ever to see Freiburg. At last we perceived it at what appeared to us the distance only of four miles, but they seemed to lengthen as we went on. More than two hours passed before we reached the town. A beautiful avenue and many fine country houses embellish its entrance. The ridge of mountains elevate themselves higher near Freiburg as if on purpose

29. "*carrie, levite*" inserted above the blank space.

to shelter this town. A charming stream runs by its side and supplies a smaller one which flows through the town and keeps it very clean. A magnificent gothic cathedral in the centre gives it a majestic appearance.

At our arrival we got our lodgings without any opposition, but we were obliged to wait for those who remained behind us. I settled matters as well as I could in order that only two should wait while the others went to their lodgings. Mine was at an Inn, where I and my companion Fontanilles were very ill received. We supped with the Innkeepers who starved us, and while they were drinking very good wine they gave us very bad beer, which we could not drink. In the meantime a post-chaise stopped at the door with an aide-de-camp of the King of Würtenberg. He no sooner had entered and noticed us than the innkeeper, through fear of this officer, sent for some wine for us. We laughed at his simplicity, and rejoiced at the lucky chance that had spared our poor purse, for we had intended to buy a bottle. The beds were very bad yet we contented ourselves with them because there was a separate one for each of us.

Next morning, after we drank our coffee, we went to the place where the carts were to be given out. What was our astonishment when we saw none of our party, though it was rather late! Perhaps they are already gone, thought I. We remained but a short time in this uncertainty, though the little Tolrá who came in at that moment changed it into a more painful one, for not being able to explain himself he told us that Mr. [Manuel] Porres had arrived at 10 in the night almost dead. Where is he? Asked I. Come with me, I'll show you, answered he. As I went towards his lodging my head was filled with a thousand dreadful ideas. I thought he was attacked by the camp-fever, which the French and Allied armies had spread through all Germany and Switzerland, but when I saw him I was calmed, for I knew that his misfortune could be immediately remedied by a bandage. But we were all astonished how it should have happened as he lay on the cart without making the least exertion. But greater wonders awaited me in the appearance of Mr. Bravo, well dressed, as well as little Tolrá, and two French gentlemen who addrest the Porres as old acquaintance. These gentlemen begged of us to rely on them for everything that our patient might want. They sent for a surgeon, who said that two or three days at least were wanted for the reestablishment of our friend.

It was now time to provide for those who were in good health, for if we remained until Mr. P. was recovered it was necessary to do it at our own expense because the town was not obliged to maintain us longer than one day, and we could not afford it. As I had more money than the rest and as I was included in the passport of Messers Porres, I thought it best to remain with them while the others should continue their journey. But Mr. Guevara, their cousin, wanted to remain with them and let me go in his place; to which I would not agree because that would put me under the necessity of changing my name for his if I was to make use of his passport. He flew into a passion, which I could not brook, and answered him with too much quickness, until the thing becoming very serious, his companions parted us and convinced him that I was in the right. This gentleman had always a kind of jealousy against me about music, because when I was leading our little orchestra I often corrected him. His jealousy had appeared in many instances but never had burst forth till now. He reproached me with my egotism during our journey. That I am an egoist I won't deny, but God knows if I behaved so during the journey. He must have attributed to egotism what I did out of mere compliance: for when any thing was to be decided nobody would give his opinion and lest the things should remain undone I always undertook to decide the questions and put in practice what was resolved upon. So that not only all the trouble fell upon me, but the blame too if the things turned out wrong. Still this was called selfishness and a desire of commanding.

When they were all gone we began to think about ourselves, and first of all we endeavoured to get the bill for lodgings for the patient prolonged. We intended to remain all four in the same house tho' we should be obliged to sleep upon the floor, but this was needless as the French gentlemen came to take Mr. Peter and me to their own houses.

I went to Count Belisle's and Mr. Peter to Comandeur Durlach's. I now learnt every particular about these gentlemen. A great number of French emigrants who never would accept of Bonaparte's amnesty remained in that town with pensions from Great Britain.[30] These gentlemen when heard that any of their fellow sufferers wanted relief joined together to make a store of every thing they could part with of clothes and money. Count Belisle was appointed distributor, and consequently he was obliged to watch the arrival of every Spaniard to provide for his wants. The four he had to deal with wanted nothing for their dress, and even we told him that we had some money for our food, but he never would let us spend it.

Countess Belisle was a very amiable lady, her children too were very fine natures. The two boys Louis and Albert had a tutor called Herr Martin, a young German extremely good-natured. Amidst this charming family I was the same as in my own house. Yet I spent the greater part of the day with the patient, who was better pleased with my nursing than with that of this brothers, for those who never have been ill are not good nurses. The accident was now the least of our patient's evil. The worst was a very bad cold he had caught some days before and which had become very serious from neglect. He had a fever, and such was his weakness that he was not able to sit upright on his bed. He wanted nothing but health, for as for the rest, had he been in his own house he could not have been better nursed than he was. Count Belisle himself administered his medicine and broth: his brothers and myself constantly nursed him: even a Catalonian lady, who had married a watchmaker from that country, came every evening to visit him. Her husband was our interpreter, and I was his sometimes, because the Messers Porres did not understand the Catalonian dialect, which was all he knew.

After a few days the ladies where our patient was lodged said that

30. There was a broad amnesty in 1802 when many *émigrés* returned to France, but those who had actively served against the revolution were still proscribed, presumably including Fernando's hosts.

they could not keep him any longer, but Count Belisle called on them and begged them only to allow him to remain in the house, for he would send his brother to a friend's, and would take upon himself to feed the patient. They agreed to the first but they would not permit the Count to feed the patient. Two days after the Count came to me and said: you know how happy I am to have you at my house, but you must acknowledge that that is the best place the patient. I shall have him brought here with one of his brothers but as I shall not in that case have room for you I have engaged one of my best friends to receive you in his. I thanked him for his attention, and acknowledged the force of his assessment. So that as soon as we could bring the Messers Porres to agree to this plan, I was introduced to the Marquis de Corbier who lived with his daughter and his old friend Marquis Dusoulier.

Nothing was spared in this house to make me comfortable and happy. If they did not completely succeed it was through my fault, for I never could eat my meals with them, without reflecting that they were poor exiles, to whom nothing was left of their former fortune, and that perhaps I was putting them to more expense than they could afford. Perhaps too I conceal under this specious subtext my pride or aversion to owing obligations in matters where money is concerned. The illness of Mr. Porres continuing longer than what we could have expected, my fears of intruding at Mr. de Corbier's augmented. I exprest them to my good hosts, who used their best endeavours to make me believe they never put themselves out of their way for me, and that should I remain the whole winter in that town they would be always as happy to keep me, as the first day. By degrees I began to feel myself at home, and resumed my former habits; I mean that I spent my day in music, reading and walking. As for music, I always played by myself and for myself; for I knew not a single musical person. The books I recall were only those concerning the French revolution and the German grammar.

My walks were the most pleasing of my employments, whether alone, or in the company of the Ladies of my acquaintance; for the environs of the town are so beautiful that even during that severe winter they were not without charm. The prospect of the Schlossberg, a mountain imminent to the town, is most magnificent. The neighbouring and still loftier mountains at each side of the town, and the course of the Rhine at a distance render it truly interesting. This was my morning walk, or rather my race for tho' the mountain is very steep, I always ran as I went up and down to get warm. My walks in the afternoon were more varied for I was often conducted by Mlle de Corbier who knew perfectly well all the environs of the town. How charming is the innocence of the manners in that country! There I walked with an unmarried lady thro' woods and over without being in the least a subject for scandal. I observed to her sometimes the apparent impropriety of our walks. Why, answered she, I would not do it in France because the manners don't allow it, but I assure you that everywhere I will trust a gentleman, and that I feel as secure by your side as I would do by my Father's. That you may, said I, for no man of feeling would dare abuse such a confidence. This was so true that I never felt the least temptation, even to take of her hand. Our conversation[31] always was that of two poor exiles united by a similarity of misfortune. I told her my sufferings during my captivity and she told me hers, and those of her family during four and twenty years, and how little expectation she had of being happier. Still, said she, if I could see my ancient masters restored to their thrones I should forget all my evils. What fervent prayers she addressed to heaven for their reestablishment!

This veneration for the royal family was, before the revolution, a characteristic quality of the French, which now can only be found among the emigrants. I witnessed a most affecting instance of this. One Sunday before breakfast we saw a carriage passing by, in which were two very remarkable Gentlemen wearing the Orange Cockade. She started at the sight, without being able to guess who they could be, no more than myself. To get some information I went to Count Belisle's. What, are they gone? said the Countess. Oh! then I can tell

31. Underneath is penciled in "(*Mui bien!!*)."

you; 'tis the Count d'Artois—and tears of joy bathed her cheeks. He has called upon my husband, continued she, but begged we would speak not speak of it until he had gone for he had not time to see every one of us.[32]

While she was speaking, the news being spread, every one of her friends entered the room to enjoy the pleasure of beholding eyes that had seen their beloved Prince. There came the good natured, impatient Baron d'Espenan, swearing that that was the first happy day he had known for 24 years; there came too the good old General de Dortan, who could not say another word than *Madame* . . . while he kissed her hand and moistened it with a tear: and there came a crowd of good old French as happy as if they had found a long-lost father. I was not an indifferent spectator—the happiness of my friends and benefactors was my own. Oh! might I have also witnessed their emotions upon the entrance of their beloved King into Paris! During this tender scene Count Belisle carried this tidings to the Corbiers, and engaged myself to dinner with us to tell us at leisure every particular of his interview with the Count d'Artois. A few days after he followed him to France and I have not seen him since.

Besides the families of Belisle and Corbier I was introduced to many other good French, such as the Comandeur de Reynach and his Niece; Count Belisle's Aunt and her daughter Adelaide, both *ci devant* Chanoinesses: Monsieur de About Justin, tho' I should not put him in the number of the good, for he was hated by all his countrymen: Monsieur Durget, a native of Franche Comté, who aspired always to be called a Spaniard because his country had once belonged to Spain: L'Abbé who was very useful to our patient: and a great number whose names I don't remember. All of them were very industrious, particularly Count Belisle and his cousin Baron d'Espenan. The latter made beautiful cages, and the former besides being his own house-

32. The Count of Artois was Louis XVI's brother and an active counterrevolutionary plotter in exile. He ascended to the throne in 1824 as Charles X after the death of his brother Louis XVIII.

keeper excelled in tapestry work.[33] As I express my surprise once at his ingenuity in this kind of work, he answered with pleasantry[34] *Je sais faire tout cela mais quand il le faut je sais faire aussi le Monsieur* [I know how to do all that, but when it is necessary I also know how to be a Gentleman]. This was true, for nobody could better assume the dignity of a man of fashion than he could: tho' he was not at all proud among his friends.

Our patient continued in the same unpromising state, while his brothers grew uneasy at seeing that we were spending our little money and becoming troublesome to our hospitable friends by our long delay. Nothing was spared to restore him but nothing succeeded. The first physician to whom we applied being not very attentive we called in a young man. Herr Carl, the friend of Herr Martin, the tutor of Count Belisle's children. This young man was reckoned very clever, but with all his skill he could do no more than what I had said: to wait until time and wholesome food should restore the strength he had lost by the hardships he had endured and by the severe cold he had caught. So we were obliged to yield to necessity and wait with patience.

But how inexplicable the ways of Providence! The very subject of our distress became a source of comforts for the continuation of our journey. A carriage, a horse and a servant were the fruit of our delay. The manner of obtaining them was as follows. One day after dinner I was sitting at the window of my hosts watching to see if any Spaniard should pass when we perceived a very neatly dressed officer on horseback followed by a kind of country carriage, called Char-a-banc, in which were two people. Mlle. de Corbier said they had the Spanish cockade, but I said they were too fine to be Spaniards. I soon, however, saw the red cockade and presently distinguished the regiment and at last I discovered my friends Andriani and Dusment.[35] I got into their

33. "*travailloit è merveille en tapisserie*" written above.

34. "*il me dit plaisamment*" written above.

35. Luis Maria Andriani y Escoffett was the military governor of Sagunto, which fell to the French in 1811, when he was taken prisoner.

carriage to direct their way about the town in which time they told me their story. These two gentlemen were the intimate friends of two ladies of fashion at Dijon, so much so that when the *dêpot* was removed from that town these ladies obtained from the government permission to keep them during their captivity at their country houses. There they remained until the Austrians entered Dijon. The Austrian Commander treated them with the highest distinction and freed the Ladies from the responsibility in which they were to the French government for the persons of these two prisoners. Nothing could then detain them in France but their friends, and these were too generous. I daresay, to keep them at the risk of seeing them again prisoners: they therefore no longer opposed their quitting France but supplied them with every thing to make them comfortable during this long journey.

I took them to the Porres, their intimate friends, and went to my usual walk. When I came back to the Porres I was surprised to hear that the carriage, horse, and servant were already our own for 200 francs payable in Spain. Our friends wished to part with all this embarrassment that they might go by the post, and as they had no want of money they were very happy to secure the value of their equipage. We made a kind of cover to the back bench of our Char-a-banc, and we bought an old mare for a trifle to help our poor horse, who was to draw five people. All these arrangements were very little approved of by me, for I never could believe that our horses were able to draw such weight. Experience proved that I was wrong and procured me many sarcasms from Mr. Peter.

I now saw with pain the moment approach in which I was to part forever with so many good friends, and throw myself upon the wider world without money or protection. But these reflections very soon gave place to encouraging ones of the pleasures that awaited me when landed on the blessed English shore: plentyful freedom and a brother's arms. But was I sure of arriving there? Was I not to pass by all the fortresses on the Rhine from which the garrisons made frequent sorties? Was I not to cross a country infected with the plague? A bold resolution was better than any reflection. I had recourse to it and gaily prepared to continue my journey. As for Mr. Manuel we took every precaution against his catching another cold. Besides having double flannel, coat and greatcoat, he had a cap and a handkerchief enveloping his whole face up to the eyes: a muff to keep his hands warm, and a large bag made of sheep's skin in which he put both his feet. He was truly ridiculous in this garb, but he was so warm in it that in spite of the severity of the cold we endured on the journey he never complained of it.

The 21st of February we bid farewell to our good friends, who could not restrain their tears. But before I proceed with my recital I must mention another advantage which our delay at Freiburg procured us. As every day there passed some Spaniard coming from France, and as we took them all to Count Belisle's to be relieved, we had daily accounts of the treatment which these prisoners had escaped. One said he had not obtained a farthing from Caamaño, another said he had, until two of our friends told us that the Spanish Ambassador to the King of Prussia whom we had met at Basel had obtained from the Government of Berne a supply of ten thousand francs to relieve the distressed Spaniards. This money was entrusted to the care of the good old General Caamaño, of whom I have already spoken. We no sooner knew of this than we began to exert ourselves to get a share in this supply. We spoke of it to our friends and found that nothing could be easier for Marquis Dusoulier was an intimate friend of Countess d'Erlach who lived at Berne in the very same house with Mr. Caamaño. We wrote to him and had Mr. d'Erlach deliver our letter and sanctioned it with our recommendation.

The result could not be doubtful: a few days before our departure we were blest with five hundred francs. Our joy upon this occasion was unutterable. My share in the 500 francs made me then happier than 500 pounds would make now.

To prevent mistakes in our further accounts Mr. Peter proposed a very simple scheme: that every one of us should put a hundred francs into a common purse from which the common expenses were to be paid. By this means the purse bearer had no occasion to keep an acct., a very troublesome thing in a journey. This employment was given to Mr. Joseph. I had for my share everything concerning papers, and Mr. Peter who is an uncommonly good whip took upon himself the business of driving and of overlooking our servant in the care of the horses. Our convalescent was exempted from any other trouble than that of taking care of himself. Matters thus settled we set off at 9 o'clock in the morning. During our way we spoke of nothing but Freiburg, and as usual among young men, we supposed each other to be in love with some of the ladies of our acquaintance and joked upon the subject to extort the truth by the manner in which the jokes should be received. As my heart was not engaged I could answer without a blush, and give joke for joke. It was not so with poor Mr. Peter. He was out of temper with our jests and only confirmed us in what we had heard from the servants, that they had seen him once stealing a kiss of the person to whom we saw him constantly devoted; a handsome woman indeed, and worthy of her lover, a high spirited Spanish nobleman.

From this we passed to other subjects, among which was the adventure of the English officer at Freiburg. As I was going once to Count Belisle's I met with a gentleman wearing a black and red cockade. I looked at it as he looked at mine, until we were sure of our conjectures. He addressed me the first in Spanish, begging leave to ask me if I was a Spaniard. I answered in the affirmative and told him I was sure he was an Englishman. Quite gratified with our meeting we agreed to drink a bottle of wine, after which I took him to the Porres. There he displayed all his good temper and his liveliness. In this style he spoke perfectly good Spanish. He was completely master of all the Spanish puns and of all the *chistes* [jests] of the familiar language, which appeared still more graceful in the mouth of a foreigner and with his own accent. Of course he had been taught by the Spanish Ladies. Gratitude perhaps for their kindness was the reason why he was so fond of them. He doted on them but, he said, he always endeavoured to hide from them that he was an Englishman; because the roughness and coldness of the English manners are not a great recommendation with the ladies.

The repetition of several other stories employed our minds during our whole way to Kaensingen [Kenzingen]. We scarcely had time to look about us, but we lost very little for the country was not at all interesting. This is perhaps the reason why I retain so little remembrance of it. On our arrival at Kenzingen we met with a large body of troops that were to pass the night there; consequently there was no room left for us, and we were obliged to go on to the neighbouring town Et[t]enheim, famous for the murder of the Duke d'Enghien.[36] He had retired to this place where he was beloved by all the inhabitants, but particularly by a noble Lady in the neighbourhood. He loved her most passionately, and could not take upon himself to leave her tho' he had many reasons to believe that Bonaparte was endeavouring to take him. He listened only to love in spite of the advice of all his friends. He soon fell the victim: the Gendarmes of Strasbourg came in the dark, stole into his house and carried him to France. The life of a Bourbon in the hands of Bonaparte was not of long duration. This single murder will cover him with eternal shame. My mind was occupied with these ideas when I entered Ettenheim and I found the inhabitants were filled with the same sentiments, which will last from generation to generation.

We were kindly received by the magistrates and got good lodgings. I was in a pleasant family; but what was my astonishment when I saw an Hebrew book! What can the man do with this, said I? I asked him if he understood it. He told me, yes. My astonishment was still greater. At supper they placed me at the furthest end of the table from which they sat, and still I wasn't aware of what they were: for such is my prejudice against Jews that I could never think a Jew could be an honest man. At last I awoke from my stupidity when I saw their ablutions. But can prejudices have such power even upon *enlightened* minds! I must acknowledge that the idea of being among Jews made me uncomfortable, tho' they were the most excellent people.

36. An émigré from one of France's most illustrious noble families, Louis-Antoine de Bourbon Condé was kidnapped at the behest of Napoleon and the secret police and brought to Vincennes, where he was convicted by a court-martial and executed in 1804.

The 22nd in the morning we left this town after having eaten our breakfast, a circumstance that seldom had taken place before, but which we meant to repeat now every day; for by this time we had gained more confidence and exacted everything from our Landlords as if we belonged to the Allied Army. We did not behave so before: first because we knew not our rights, and secondly because we had so little appearance of gentlemen, that nobody would respect us. But now we had a carriage and servant and had dressed Mr. Peter in the most dazzling military uniform and everybody paid us all sort of attentions.

In our way to Offenburg we met with nothing worth repeating, or rather I may say I keep very little remembrance of it. What is still present to my recollection is the town. It is small and not pretty. It is surrounded by some fortifications and there was a garrison on account of the vicinity of Strasbourg. We called on the Comandant de Place for lodgings. He took our marche-route, wrote upon it the two next stages and gave it back to us, without giving us lodgings in spite of all our clamours. He said he had no room in the town and that we ought to go to the next village, Windschleguen [Windschläg], where there were no troops.

All out of temper with this injustice we pursued our way to the village. It was a small one, off the road and so near Strasbourg that the French sometimes neared up to it for the sake of plunder. I cursed a thousand times the Commandant for having thus endangered so much our lives and liberty but there was no help for it was too late to go farther. I wanted to drown my uneasiness in wines but I was told they kept no good wine in the place because nothing was safe in it. In short, everything bespoke my danger. The Bürgermeister was a poor peasant who could not write nor speak anything but German but when he saw we were Spaniards he sent for a young man who spoke good Spanish. I was lodged afterwards in his house and had a long conversation with him. He was a Butcher and under this business followed the French army to Spain: he remained there a long while, and made a great deal of money, but when the army retired he lost it all and brought home nothing but a sabre wound. I cannot complain of these poor people for they gave me of the best they had, tho' their best was not very good. The Porres were with me until the time of going to bed. My own was a straw bed upon the floor, raised a little at one end by a chair turned topsy-turvy, and thin feather bed to cover myself with. The room was cold because the fire in the stove was out; and my bed was not well adapted to keep me warm. This reason alone would have kept me awake, but besides that the danger in which I was of falling again into the hands of the French drove away even the idea of sleep. How long is a winter's night in such anxiety! My watch told me when it was time to set off rather earlier than usual. We hurried from that place at the time when the inhabitants had retired from their dancing for it was the last day of carnival.

Mr. Peter had taken it into his head that our horses were able to go two stages every day, and tho' I could not believe it we were to try it that day, the 23rd. This plan, besides its greater expedition, had another advantage, that of getting two rations every day for our horses, and two meals for ourselves. We arrived at Bühl by dinnertime. The Commissary of this small and ugly town willingly gave us a billet for dinner, for he saw we could have exacted lodgings also. The billets were directed to two inns where we got a tolerable good dinner. In this part of Germany the butchers are all innkeepers. They send their children to France to learn both their business and the French language; for no innkeeper can carry on his business without knowing this language.

The next stage was a very short one in so much that we arrived at Rastadt [Rastatt] still gay with the steams of the wine of our dinner and the *schnapps* (the name by which any kind of spirits was understood in the Allied army) of our dessert.

Rastatt is a town of a particular shape, which I have seen only in Germany, where they are very common—extremely wide streets, low houses but regular, and a great number of large buildings. The squares are so large that it is impossible to distinguish anybody from the opposite side. Of this shape are also [K]arlsruhe and particularly Darmstadt. As these towns are quite new built I fancy this is the modern taste for building in that country, which agrees with my taste, besides being very healthy.

We thought when we were in so large a town as Rastatt there could be no want of room for us. In this persuasion I was happy to have come two stages that day. We ran about all the town in search of the *Platz-Comandant,* as the Germans call him, and after all we unluckily found a Prussian Officer who very uncivilly told us he had nothing to do with us, and that we ought to apply to the Commissary. I say unluckily because there was another Commandant as we have since learnt, who spent his time in a Coffee-house smoking and drinking, and was extremely fond of Spaniards. This man whenever the Commissary refused them lodgings gave such positive orders that the Commissary was obliged to comply. For this reason the Commissary had a great dislike to us. He was not in his office when we called. His clerk was very polite but when the Commissary came we saw a different man. He took our marche-route without speaking a word, wrote down in it the successive stages to Frankfurt, and gave us a billet to get lodgings in the next village, called Bitiheim [Bietigheim], a name connected with the greatest hardships perhaps that I have ever endured. No reasoning could move him, and in spite of its being almost dark, our horses overcome with the double stage, and ourselves benumbed with cold, we were obliged to go on to Bietigheim.

Two miles beyond Rastatt we met with two young recruits to whom we show'd our billet. They looked at it and pointed out to us the way and their own billet so as to make us understand that all of us were directed by the Commissary to the same village. This pleased me much because the young men would conduct us, which they did very willingly across fields and meadows, with great difficulty to our horses. At last we reached the village and the Bürgermeister's Office, but the worst was awaiting us for that village was not Bietigheim. There I burst into a fit of the most violent passion against the Commissary, and the stupid recruits, that had so awkwardly misled us, lengthening our way 3 miles more. I asked for somebody to conduct us to the place of our destination but the peasant who came with us for this purpose would not proceed beyond the limits of his Village. He pointed out to us the way, and unmoved by prayers or offers he flew back to his supper. It was dark, extremely cold and we had to go through an enclosed and unknown way so rough with the frozen mud that our horses could hardly draw on the char-a-banc tho' only two of us were within it. I was walking and shuddering with cold and rage, for both easily got the better of me, and under those circumstances few would have resisted them.

When we reached Bietigheim it was so cold and dark that no peasant was to be found to direct us to the Bürgermeister's. If we knocked at the doors nobody would answer from the terror they were in of the Cossacks. This put me so much out of temper that I swore I would force the first peasant I met with to conduct me to the Bürgermeister's. One immediately appeared, whom I caught hold by the arm, saying to him at the same time in my bad German and with a threatening tone: *Comen sie mis mier nach Bourgmaister* [Take me to the mayor]. I did not wait for his answer but obliged him to comply with my wish. The poor wretch obeyed and conducted us to the Bürgermeister. This was a stupid yet malicious peasant, whom we could not understand not being able to speak anything but bad German. I was obliged to transact all the business. His room was quite warm at which I began to recover my temper and fancy that everything was to continue as I wished it—a clean and bountiful supper and a warm bed.

How disappointed was I when I entered my lodgings and saw a filthy house swarming with filthy women, one of whom abused me in her language while she was taking my billet. I had scarcely sat down when she came to me in the most violent manner crying out to me *Kein fleisch, kein wein* (no meat, no wine) to which I in the same tone answered: *abendessen, abendessen* (supper, supper). I endeavoured to make her understand that I was not a common soldier as she believed, and perhaps for this reason she complied in giving me a supper. What supper, gracious God! I think I could have starved rather than have eaten it: some sour milk in which she had steeped some bread blacker than my hat and a kind of nasty stuff which I was at a loss to find a name for. My gestures and words made everyone aware of my distracted situation, in so much that every one in the house was silent except the landlady and I. When I saw that nothing was to be expected I gave money to get wine and potatoes, upon which I made my supper, tho' both wine and potatoes were extremely bad.

By this time the landlord came home and the scene was changed, tho' not more favorably to me. He was a very good-tempered man as it appeared by the good humour in which he put all the family, his wife excepted. To the former silence succeeded a perpetual chatter and laughing, which lasted till one o'clock in the morning, at which time they gave up spinning.

After my supper I called for my bed. They made it in the very room where they were sitting. It was composed of some straw upon the floor and the landlord's greatcoat but the worst was when I saw a sick person in the next room from whom they had taken a dirty pillow for my bed. This was enough to make anyone uncomfortable for it was most likely this person was infected with the plague. I was so overcome with fatigue that I threw myself upon the bed regardless of what might happen. It was of no use for the noise of the family prevented me from sleeping until they left the room. How much I suffered during this time! but this gave me the opportunity of noticing a custom which I afterwards found was the same in all the houses of German peasants in which I have been. They have but one fire in the house which serves in the kitchen to cook and to warm the stove of the sitting room. By this they remain as long as possible because the straw and a cold room that awaits them when they go to sleep is worse than to sit up almost all night in a warm room: but the oddest thing of all is that every one of them, not even women excepted, undress themselves, as far as German decorum will allow, leave their clothes in the sitting room, and so half-naked, without shoes or stockings they run away to their straw. Very early in the morning they come back in the same garb, and dress themselves by the stove.

When I was left to myself I thought I might enjoy some sleep, but now the fire being out the cold tormented me so much that I could hardly sleep. In the morning the children came up to my bed playing and teasing me and thus preventing me from getting a little rest now that the fire was again lighted. It was no wonder if the cold had made me suffer so bitterly when the very inhabitants could hardly resist it. Everyone in the house came to me saying *Viel cold* (very cold).

I had some sour milk and potatoes for my breakfast, after which in the greatest state of despondency I went to meet my companions. These two hard nights and the probability that the ensuing would be as bad destroyed all hope within me. I shall be frozen before I reach England said I; but who could have told me that the happiest, the most comfortable night I ever had known was to be that very say same day month [*sic*]! My sufferings were so visible in my face that my companions could not help pitying me. In this state of despondency I started from Bietigheim the 24th in the morning in one of the coldest days of that winter. Our direction was to Durlach to which there are two ways. We missed the shortest and luckily took the one passing through Karlsruhe, the residence of the Duke of Baden. In spite of all my sufferings, which had been increasing during the way on account of the high and cold wind I could not help admiring the beauty of the avenue leading to this handsome town, and the magnificence of the Parks adjoining it. As I approached the town, languid from want of food and stiff with cold, running on foot to get warm with my congealed breath covering my mustaches and whiskers; I had an opportunity of comparing my situation with that of the Duke of Baden who passed by me in a magnificent carriage and six; preceded and followed by many outriders dressed in the most elegant manner. Who would not change my situation for his? Yet I am sure he was more miserable than I was for just at that time his wife[37] had got into a scrape, by meddling in a conspiracy against the interests of the Allies: and tho' it was not as yet evident he was not much trusted by them.

37. Stephanie, grand duchess of Baden, was Stephanie Beauharnais, niece of the Empress Josephine and Napoleon's adopted daughter. She married Karl, the hereditary prince of Baden, in 1806.

It was not allowed to exact lodgings or rations in this town but in consideration to me, my companions agreed to eat our dinner at our own expense. We entered a well looking Inn. The dining room was full of military men of the garrison. Many of them knew us to be Spaniards and addressed us in Spanish to our great astonishment. The warmth of the room and the hope of a comfortable and clean dinner roused my almost exhausted spirits and enabled me to speak to this people. They belonged to the corps of Baden troops, which had been three years in Spain under Bonaparte. This corps or rather its wrecks was recalled for the campaign of Russia and followed the general defection of the German troops from Bonaparte. The fondness for the Spanish women is the general topic of foreigners who have been in that country: yet there was before us an instance of what I have observed in my travels—that in every country the sex is gifted with loveliness, for two of the maids were most charming girls. The military men cheated them in the Spanish they had taught them. For instance they said *dame un bezo* [give me a kiss], believing they said, give me bread, and many other of this kind. I endeavoured to confirm them in these innocent errors and some of my own to the great amusement of the customers of the house. The conversation with the girls, the good dinner and above all the nice white wine of the country made me forget all my past hardships, so much so that even my friends could hardly believe it. They themselves were not very sober, as appeared when we began our journey for Mr. Peter drove with such speed that we past even post chaises, tho' we had afterwards to complain of him for from this time our poor mare became lame.

Before I left Karlsruhe I went to see the Palace. It occupies one side of a magnificent Square, superior to any as there in London both in size and in regularity of the buildings, tho' for the rest it was not so cheerful as the English Sqres., not having any garden in the center.

The road from this town to Durlach is eight miles but lined the whole way with beautiful trees and in a strait line. In Durlach, an old town tho' not ugly, we were received by the magistrates in the kindest manner. We were lodged in very good houses and without any delay.

My Landlord was School Master, extremely good and kind, as was all his family. They were much pleased to see the pleasure I took in speaking German and taught me as much of it as they could in so short a time. I wonder how I could make myself understood, but certainly we held a conversation without any intermission for 4 or 5 hours and all in German. The two most essential phrases I learned there were *Ich glaube nix: Is kein mechlik. I do not believe it: It is impossible.* I say essential because we were obliged to employ them to almost all the Bürgermeisters when they told us they had no carts nor lodgings to give us, which happened very often.

When I had taken some fruit at the school master's, I went to Mr. Manuel, who accompanied me to Mr. Peter's. He was in an excellent Inn among some very lively girls but they could not speak with them as he was ignorant of the German. As soon as I came, my spirits enlivened with the wine of Karlsruhe and that of the School Master's I began a conversation in German, more pleasing to them than that of the best German scholar. They were musicians—I sang them German songs and begged they would teach me the words, which I could not obtain from them, neither could I prevail on them to let me hear them play.

I left them soon and went to my lodgings for supper. There I met the eldest son of the Master, who gave me a lesson of German handwriting. Afterwards we played flute duets and talked German till very late. My bed was comfortable and of an odd shape, which I do not remember whether I have described. There is but one sheet, and instead of blankets and counterpane there is nothing but a feather bed covered with a linen case serving as an upper sheet.

Next morning, the 25th February, after I had drank my coffee we set off to Langenbrüken. As far as I can recollect the road goes through an uneven country, deviating a little from the course of the Rhine, and through several large towns which names I do not know. Nothing worthy of notice happened in our way. My usual lowness of spirits came on again and I wished for nothing but repose, tho' it was very far from me, for we had formed the plan to reach Heidelberg: consequently we meant only to eat our dinner at Langenbrüken. This proved to be an ugly Village inhabited by people almost savage, yet I cannot complain for I was sent with Mr. Manuel to one of the principal houses where we had a good dinner. It must be acknowledged, however, that the vicinity of the Landlady who was very ill with the plague made our dinner rather uncomfortable: but I was thinking how much more so she necessarily must be to see in us intruders, the cause of her illness, for the plague had been communicated by the Allied army. I hurried my dinner and went to join Mr. Peter where he was dining. He had not been so lucky as myself and therefore had very soon done, and got in readiness to pursue our journey.

The road now gets again to the course of the Rhine and by the foot of the ridge of mountains, which border this River. The beauty of this charming situation increases as we approach Heidelberg. The vale widens, the mountains become higher, and the road winds through a better cultivated country, still lined with cherry trees. We could not enjoy in their full extent all their beauties because it was rather dark when we reached the town. We had no idea of its extent nor position, and thought that it was small, in which opinion we were confirmed by not discovering anything of it when by our calculations we guessed it to be near. Our astonishment was therefore the greatest when upon turning a mountain we saw that magnificent town. *Padre Magres, cabemos aqui?* [Padre Magres, is there room for us here?] asked Mr. Joseph of me. I believe not, said I, for it had proved a constant rule that in the large towns they sent us to a neighbouring village. We therefore jokingly said when we saw a large town—*aqui no cabemos* [there is no room for us here].

It was now quite dark and we knew not to whom to apply, at last we were directed to the Commissary, a very civil man. Everything was settled by him in a short time. He gave us our bills and people to show us the houses. I could not believe we were right when our leader knocked at the door, so grand was its appearance. But it was so, and my astonishment still increased when the Lady herself came down to make us her excuses in the most polite manner for not receiving us in her own house *Mais soyez persuadés, Messieurs,* said she, *que je n'epargneras rien pourque vous ne regretiez pas ma maison* [Rest assured, gentlemen, I will spare nothing so that you won't regret not being in my home]. She was as good as her word. Our guide shewed us to the coffee house which she named. Her name alone was our best recommendation for no sooner did the Landlord hear it than he begged us a thousand pardons for being obliged to make us wait a moment while he was engaged with some Spanish gentlemen just arrived at his house. Spanish gentlemen! said I. Let us see them. It was exactly what I guessed—our companions had been lodged in the same coffee house. How happy we were to meet anybody may easily conceive. Supper was not ready nor was it in less than two hours. We passed all this time in the coffee room overlooking the card tables. I could not understand the game but amused myself in observing the manners of the Germans and the oddity of their cards. They are twice the size of the English ones and the figures have no legs but the upper part of the body is instead of them, so that in whatever manner you may catch hold of the card the figure is upright.

At last supper was ready. We were shown into a nice dining room where a table served on in the most delicate manner awaited us. The two owners of the house waited upon us, and it was truly shameful for they looked more of the gentlemen than ourselves. After the first course they gave us a quantity of stewed fruits, by which we understood the supper was finished but very soon we perceived our error, for after the stewed fruits we had another course more splendid than the first, and a fine dessert. Our keen appetite and the exquisiteness of the meats made us eat so much as to attract the notice of the French gentlemen supping with us.

Their beds did not correspond with the supper. Mine was made upon a Sopha, and confined in such a manner that I could scarcely sleep. A nice breakfast awaited us after we had been examining all that beautiful town. It stands upon rising ground and overlooks a river called [Neckar], which joins the Rhine a few miles beyond. The bridge over it is very fine. We past it the 26th to go to Heppenheim and no farther to rest our horses.

This town is an old, irregular small one: nothing but misery appears in it and much more so to our eyes accustomed to the sight of Heidelberg. The mansion house is a large old building in the highest part of the town within the [blank] of a very old fortification. The Mayor was a clown giving himself the airs of an important being. He delivered the bills with great solemnity, but the houses to which they were directed did not answer to it, for they were most wretched, tho' the owners proved very good people. As we arrived early we were very much annoyed by the filth of our lodgings. The best of them was a baker's and there we assembled until it was time to go to bed. Mine was extremely filthy, and in a room excessively cold. I could not sleep but when I was beginning to dose I awoke at the sound of many trumpets or horns playing in a most lamentable manner. This sound happened to coincide with the noise of numerous cart and horses crossing the town with great rapidity. All these things combined occasioned me great uneasiness, for I never forgot that all the fortresses upon the Rhine had very good garrisons and that they made frequent sorties. Yet I thought the best was to sleep, and I endeavoured to do so. The horns continued the same during the whole night but by the combination of the number of sounds they gave with the hours of the clock I discovered they were no more than watchmen, who in that part of Germany, tell the hour with horns instead of crying it out as in other countries. My bed was so uncomfortable that I was not averse to getting up in the morning. The stars were still shining when I called for my coffee and it was very lucky for as we intended to reach Francfort sur le Mein [Frankfurt] that day it was necessary to set off early. I awoke my companions and hurried them out of this unpleasant town.

I do not recollect the particulars of our journey during the morning only that it was very cold and fine. By twelve o'clock we reached Darmstadt, the Capital of the Dukedom of Hesse Darmstadt, the description of which I have already given in that of Rastatt. I shall only add the prodigious wideness of its streets and squares. The lowness of the buildings, however, makes them appear more so, but yet there are some in which I could not have distinguished any acquaintance passing on the other side of the way. The approach of this town is very handsome on account of the number of gardens and villas near it. The ground is very level and yet the country is pretty. At that time the town was very lively, because they were organizing a numerous body of troops, and that was the place for their meeting. Their appearance was very good—fine men and well dressed and armed but all new soldiers. Tho' we were ragged, they looked at us with a kind of veneration, owing to our seniority in the profession.

We applied to the Russian Plaz-Commander to have an order for our bills. He did not like our visit for he had better company—a beautiful young woman—his wife perhaps or something else. Her eyes were always fixed on him, and sometimes she came behind him while he was writing and leaned upon his shoulders. My obdurate heart felt nothing of this interesting scene. What a burthen for a soldier, said I, to carry with him a woman! Could he not find women in his way? Are they not all alike? How mistaken was I! If the poor Russian had in his heart, or rather in his mind, a certain complaint with which I was not acquainted, they would not be all alike, nay, there would be but one woman in the world.

With the Russian's order we went to the mansion for our bills. We were told by the porter of the mansion to remain in his room while he went to get our bills. In this time we examined a specimen of the swords of the ancient Germans. It was six or seven feet long and broad in proportion without an edge and was to be used with both hands, yet with both mine I could scarcely lift it up. Must mankind decay in physical strength as it improves in mental faculties!

Our bill was only for dinner for we intended to go to Frankfurt the same day. It included all of us, so we dined together in an Inn of the first description, tho' the dinner was rather scanty. Some military men whom we thought officers introduced themselves to us in the dining room. We were pleased with their politeness and engaged in conversation. We learned from them that they were common soldiers in which rank almost all the high classes of the country had engaged themselves, out of patriotism. Their appearance therefore was not like that of common soldiers. Their hatred against the French domination cannot be expressed nor their esteem for the conduct of the Spaniards during the war. But this esteem is common to all the nations of Europe, English and Spaniards excepted. Among these two nations only may be found people who would not acknowledge the merit of the unexampled resistance of the Spaniards.[38]

The beginning of the road to Frankfurt is a beautiful Avenue of majestic trees. I walked the greatest part of the way on account of the cold. The ground now began to be rather uneven for we had deviated from the course of the Rhine. We crossed many woods of fir on a sandy soil. All that part looked colder than the rest. Upon some hills the ice tho' constantly trodden by a numerous army was as hard as stone, while in other roads the passing of the army had reduced the ice to dust. As we went up a mountain a mile distant from Frankfurt we discovered this town situated on the right bank of the Main. This river flows through a vast plain and discharges itself into the Rhine a few miles beyond the town. The prospect of any large town from a height has a charm and much more if a river runs by it. This is the case with Frankfurt in approaching it by the side of Darmstadt. I had time to examine it with leisure for the road winds down to the town very gently. Those hills were very pleasant before the last *déroute* [rout] of the French, but when after the battle of Leipzig they encamped here for a few days they destroyed everything. The Main and its bridge at

38. Fernando's comments aptly capture the distrust and dislike between the Spanish and British, which was widely reflected in British military correspondence and memoirs of the Peninsular War. For example, Gavin Daly notes that, after the setbacks at Corunna and Talavera in 1809, "there was a strong sense [among the British] of Spanish perfidy: that the Spanish nation, from its generals down to its peasants, could not be relied upon to support the British army" (*The British Soldier in the Peninsular War: Encounters with Spain and Portugal, 1808–1814* [New York, Palgrave Macmillan, 2013], 107). Such attitudes persisted to the war's very end, with a British officer writing that "you may rely on it that no two nations are more opposite in every particular than the Spaniards and the English and no two Armies can detest each other more" (William Bragge, quoted ibid., 129).

this place are grand but the entrance of the town gives not a favourable impression of it. The streets in this part are narrow and crooked, the buildings high and shabby, very unlike the center of the town.

We asked the Officer on duty at the gate to spare us a soldier to show us to the Russian Commandant. It was a long way to go, and when we were there we had the disappointment to hear that we ought to have applied to the Austrian Commandant. He was a fat, good-natured fellow, with whom we had very soon settled our matters. He granted us privilege to stay in the town for three days and told us to call next day for our Marche-Route. As we were going out we met a friend whom we could never have expected to see. His name is Juan Nepomuceno Sarabia. He had attempted escaping a few days before us, but had failed in his scheme and had returned to Chalon where he applied to Desgranges. Savoje undertook to guide him and others, and lost his way as he did with us, but this time he lost his courage also and compelled them to remain a whole day in a wood without any food after they had been walking all the preceding night. He had met after this with many other adventures. Now he was in the company of some young Dutch gentlemen whom Bonaparte had forced to serve in the *Garde d'honneur,* and were now going home after they had deserted Napoleon. Mr. Sarabia was not the only acquaintance we met with at Frankfurt for the town was crowded with Spaniards, a number of Scoundrels among them.

But let us not anticipate anything. A soldier from the Austrian Commandant conducted us to the Mansion, where we met with many difficulties to get the rations for our horses. It was night before we procured them and in such a large town it was impossible to find out our lodgings, but some charitable Jews for the sake of a few *kreutzers* took the trouble to be our guides. Notwithstanding their knowledge of the town we roamed an hour before we were settled in our houses. Mine was a magnificent one. The maid showed me into an upper room in which there was no fire. I could not remain without one and consequently went downstairs with the resolution to sit with the Master of the house, but as I was opening the door of the drawing room the maid all confused at my boldness would not let me enter. I said I wanted to speak to the Master but with such emphasis that a Gentleman came to me to know what I wanted. As he spoke French I explained to him who I was and my claims to their fire. He went back to the lady and my admittance was granted. What was my confusion when in the filthy state in which my clothes were I found myself among a nice and numerous party of young ladies and gentlemen! The latter came by turns to speak to me out of politeness. I was quite aware of my intrusion and begged to have a fire in my room to take a little rest. During this time I was observing their manners. They were drinking tea the same as in England, but the freedom between the sexes showed them to be German. However, I must own that they were almost all relations. When I thought my fire was lit up I took leave of the Lady and went to my room. There I enjoyed a complete liberty: I ate my supper by myself, drank many a bumper and went to my bed happier than I shall go by and by.

Next morning after a careful toilet I called on my companions with a design of making some bargains. I wanted a sword, a Russian cap and levite [a loose garment]. As my stock of money was very small, everything appeared to me too expensive, and therefore after having been a shopping all the morning I bought only the cap. We were told of an English Colonel employed as they said by his government to forward the Spaniards to their own country. We called on him thinking he was going to give us everything but he had nothing in his power but to prolong our stay in Frankfurt and as he said in his broken Spanish: *Me tiene mucho barcos en la Haya para pasa Vm. en Inglaterra* [Me have many boats in The Hague so that you can go in England]. How far this was true will appear in the sequel.[39] He was nothing more than one of those numerous Agents of the British Government to inspect the operations of the Allied Army. He had commanded a Spanish regiment, and lost a hand at Leipzig. We parted very good friends but did not accept of his offer to remain a few days more. It was truly

39. "*par la suite*" written above "sequel."

shameful to see how this town swarmed with officers of all nations who under trifling pretexts abandoned their corps to enjoy themselves in plenty and safety. The inhabitants of this abuse were overwhelmed with military lodgers, whom they were also obliged to feed.

My Landlord had at that time an Austrian besides myself. We met at dinner at which time I became acquainted with the family. It was composed of two brothers and a sister all living in a commercial association. And a pleasant family indeed. They were musical, especially the youngest brother. He played very well the piano-forte and sung still better. After dinner I took a walk with my companions and went to a farrier to consult him about our mare, which was very ill. He with great solemnity wrote in Latin a prescription and swore it was a secret known only to himself. He was, however, so kind as to give us his secret for half a guinea. We spend the evening drinking punch and parted to meet next morning to pursue our journey.

The 1st of March we set off for Königstein. The way to it is through a barren tract without any road. We were obliged to enquire of every person whom we met for the way to Königstein, and yet after wandering a long time we reached a Village where we learnt we were wrong. Nothing was right that day; the road very bad, our humour worse, and our horses ill and not well shod. From this Village the way is over mountains where nothing but stones is to be seen. A cold foggy weather gave a more melancholy turn to my mind. By two o'clock we reached a village we took for Königstein. We met there with a party of Spaniards, which confirmed us in our error, but when we showed our passport to the Bürgermeister we had the disappointment of hearing that our destination was 6 miles further. The way was worse and worse and our spirits much more so. Some wretched French prisoners whom we met half starved increased my melancholy for they reminded me of the time when I was in their case. I remembered how most of the French had insulted my misery, and how humiliated they were now. Tomorrow I may be a prisoner again, said I, and compassion for those wretches was my predominant feeling.

This miserable town of Königstein is nothing but a small Village laid waste by the Cossacks. A soldier therefore was a curse to every inhabitant. Their character too like that of all the inhabitants of the County of Nassau is uncommonly rough and savage, so that we were received in the most uncivil manner. We behaved the same in speaking to the Bürgermeister, who would not give us the rations for our horses. We spoke among ourselves in Spanish, while a clown was looking at us with a malicious air. How surprised were we when we heard him take a part in our conversation in Spanish! He proved as great a rogue as all those foreigners who have been long in Spain. We would obtain nothing but our lodgings, and these so bad that I regretted many others which I had deemed very bad during our journey. The people of my house were two old sickly women who caused me nausea to look at them. The dinner they gave me was as loathsome as themselves. Mr. Joseph was as bad off as myself, his house was opposite to mine and so near that I called him from my window after supper to drink half a bottle of wine that I had bought to drive away melancholy. We sat till late engaged in a delightful conversation, the effect of his esteem for me, for where he was not attached he was so particularly reserved that his voice was scarcely heard in society. He was endowed with great mental powers but the diffidence of his character prevented the display of him.[40]

Next day we intended to go two stages further tho' the road and the weather were rather unfavourable. Some Flemish wagoners who came the road we were going feared that the mountains could not be passed on account of the snows. In fact, when we got to the summit of them we apprehended more than once that we should be lost in the snows. I took such particular notice of this wild country not to miss the track that I can remember the whole of it as well as if I was seeing it now. Some parts of it are really picturesque, especially a wood in

40. Fernando himself rewrote much of these two sentences, which originally read, "We sat till late in a delicious conversation caused by the esteem in which he had me for without that he was so particularly reserved that his voice was scarcely heard in society. He was endowed with great mental powers but . . . [original inked out]."

a steep in which the echo was so loud as to become awful. Half way from [Bad] Camberg we found a small village from whence the road is exceedingly good and free from snow as that part is comparatively low and therefore warmer.

We reached Bad Camberg by noon where we easily obtained lodgings to eat our dinner and then continue on our journey. Mr. Manuel and I went to an Apothecary's, where we met with a kind reception. A gentleman was attracted by the sound of my flute (which I always took out as soon as I entered my lodgings) who proved very useful to us for as he was the Secretary of the bailiff, he obtained the rations for our horses.

Very distressful news had by that time reached the country. Some regiments of Nassau, which Napoleon had taken into Spain deserted him and obtained leave from the Spaniards to be sent home but were all shipwrecked on the coast of Holland.

Bad Camberg is on old, ugly-looking town like all in Nassau. It is situated on a rising ground and enclosed by an old wall. The thaw had taken place all over the country and the roads were therefore very bad. At a few miles from Bad Camberg is [blank], a celebrated place for some mineral waters. The buildings for the use of them are very handsome, the only thing perhaps that has not a shabby appearance in all the County.

A few miles before you reach Limburg the country is very even but elevated and continued so until we discovered the town. A great number of horses were going by a road parallel to ours, and we learnt that they were going for the siege of Mayence [Mainz]. Limburg compared with the other towns of Nassau is a handsome one. There are many fine churches among which a Cathedral with a numerous Chapter of Canons, most respectable men.[41] Everything was settled here in a moment, the only difficulty was in reaching our lodgings for nothing can be more steep and rugged than the streets leading to them.

I was lodged in the house of a Canon as well as Mr. Manuel and Mr.

41. Another reference to his brother Joseph's career in Seville before his flight to London.

Joseph. I was received most uncivilly by the housekeeper, but as she showed me into a room where there was a good bed I did not care for the rest. After I had left my little parcel there and begged the old maid to prepare something for my supper, I went to see my companions. I spent half an hour with them and went home, but nobody answered tho' I rung the bell for a long while. This made me very uneasy for I feared that the housekeeper would not open the door out of malice. This appeared evident to me when half an hour afterwards I rung and rung without any answer. At last in the evening the door was opened to me and my supper ready, the maid having been out all that time to buy the necessaries. I had just begun my supper when the Canon entering my room addressed me in Latin. I asked him if he spoke French but upon his answering in the negative I made up my mind to venture on my broken Latin. We understood each other perfectly well as the Germans pronounce the Latin with little difference from the Spaniards. He said he would not keep me company, it being a fast day but he hoped that after supper I would accept of a bottle of wine in his room. His wine was very good and our Latin conversation so interesting that we sat up very late and parted with regret. His application of ancient words to modern objects was really laughable. For instance he called the Commissary *Satrapa* [Satrap].

How deliciously I slept in that clean bed! Next morning very early I was obliged to leave it, not to find another like it for many days. We met at Mr. Peter's, who told us the lamentable story of his landlady. She ran out of the house at the first appearance of the Cossacks in the town: it was very frosty and she slipt and broke her leg, thus encountering a real evil for the sake of avoiding an imaginary one.

The Satrap of Limburg had marked in our marche-route many places as if all of them were stages, at least we believed it so, which pleased us for we could get rations at every one of them, and good fodder for our horses. The first trial was at a wretched village called Wallmerod[er], a few miles from Limburg. Some Spaniards we met there told us that the Bürgermeister was of so sour a disposition that he had denied them the day after all kind of supplies both to continue their journey or to remain there but as they had a woman with them they could not go without carts, and had been obliged to send somebody to Limburg to get redress against this churlish Bürgermeister. We found him a savage rustic stubborn to the greatest degree. We thanked him by our gestures accompanied by the word *caput*, meaning destruction of any kind, pronounced most emphatically, but nothing could shake him. He said no to everything. As there was another village some miles further called Freilingen we drove there through the most miserable country I have ever seen.

When we arrived we met with the same obstinacy from the Bürgermeister. We feared to be received in the same manner at the next village, Wallerode [Wahlrod], so we made up our minds to get our dinner here at our own expense in the Post-house. It was a bad one and so was the wine, for which we paid near 1/2 a crown a bottle, an extravagant price comparatively to the prices of other things in that country. We hurried from this place and pursued our journey through this barren country. The road is very bad and uneven; many brooks run across it without any bridge to pass them. Throughout the whole country there is no mark of civilization and I shall not hesitate to say that the parts of Nassau I am acquainted with in all respects [are] far behind Spain, tho' Spain be called a barbarous country.

At about dark we reached Wahlrod, as miserable a Village as any of the preceding and governed by a Bürgermeister as brutal as any of the others: yet he was obliged to do his duty and give us lodgings and rations, but not without half an hour's quarrelling in my usual ridiculous manner, which was to speak all in Spanish, except the few words I knew of German. For instance, I said then *Vm. es un tunante, Señor Bourgmaister, y Ich glaube nich[t] que no tenga tapen, haver und hay. Ya es nacht y no puedo k[e]in gehe. Aquí, aquí logier [loger], que no soy k[e]in soldaten sino ofitzier, ofitzier [offizier]*. [You are a rascal, Mr. Mayor, and I do not believe that you have no *tapen, haver und hay.* It is night and I cannot leave. Here, here lodge, I am not a soldier but an officer, officer.] In this language, I always spoke and made myself understood upon any subject.

When we had obtained our lodgings and rations I felt comfortable tho' the houses of the village did not promise any comforts. Filthy and disagreeable as mine was yet it belonged to a rich peasant, and no wonder if he was so as he had kept the public house of the village for many years. By his communication with travelers perhaps he had acquired a little more civilisation than most of his countrymen. I was so pleased with this that after we had eaten our supper I engaged him to drink a bottle of wine in the public house. My civility pleased him vastly and he endeavoured to pay me every kind of attention. I must not forget that at this time I began to feel that indifference and carelessness which lasted me til now that I am become a merchant. Tho' I had but little money, I felt no inclination to save. My fondness for information had lost a great deal of its eagerness and the thoughts of forgetting my mathematics no longer troubled me: my only object was to enjoy myself as much as I could, especially in drinking, and from this day I lost no opportunity of drinking punch, my favorite beverage.[42] I cannot account for this fit, and think it very lucky that I have got rid of it, for if once my wicked nature is not checked, there is no stopping her. I have many instances of it in my former life. When shall I be reasonable!

Quite happy with my bottle of wine I went to what they were pleased to call my bed, tho' it did not look at all like a bed. I slept pretty well and awoke in good spirits to set out next morning the 4th of March. The country continued still the same and tho' the town we met with at a few miles from Wahlrod was larger than the preceding villages, yet it did not wear a better appearance. After this town the country is very mountainous and the road so bad that it was difficult to distinguish it, so much so that frequently we had like to have been lost. By nine we reached Wayerbuch [Weyerbusch], a small village but in which the people began to look less brutish. We obtained very

42. Punch became popular in England and Europe in the seventeenth century; it was associated with India and later with West Indian rum. Served warm, it combined rum or brandy with sugar, lemon, spices, and tea.

easily rations for our horses. As for ourselves we ate some bread and drank a kind of spirits made from plums like that of Liestal. Two poor Russian soldiers stopped to look at us in this village, attracted by the shining garb of Mr. Peter. We spoke to them for half an hour with great satisfaction on both sides. An old soldier is always an interesting object and their medals, their scars, and their fresh wounds proved them to be by no means new to their profession. Who would not be moved in looking at the marks and remunerations of valor, which they showed both against the Turks and the French! In taking leave of us they made us the military salute with their musquets with exceedingly good grace and boldness.

We pursued our journey to Ukerode [Uckerath], noticing with pleasure that the country began to improve as well as the roads. This small village is pretty neat and rich, for all the houses looked comfortable at least to eyes accustomed to see Wallmeroder [and] Freilingen. I dined at a kind of inn with the landlady and two passengers, but they behaved with such civility and circumspection that I thought they were guests like myself. My companions were in very respectable houses. We did not stay long for we wanted to reach Sie[g]burg but before we set off we were introduced to a Surgeon who had been in Spain with the French army.

The road is now very fine. It leads from the heights in which Uckerath stands to an immense plain, highly cultivated but so melancholy looking that my soul took a gloomy turn. In this plain are some detached hills like sugar loafs really looking as if they had been brought there by the hand of man. One of them was in former times the Citadel of Siegburg, in the others are situated very picturesque villages. At the distance of two miles from Siegburg we crossed a small river in a boat kept for that purpose, there being no bridge. The Bürgermeister of this town was an old Gentleman governed by his young wife. She acted her husband's part better than him; tho' both were civil and complaisant to us. I was sent to a Coffee house where I was surprised to see a great number of French officers. I could not forbear showing them the same haughtiness they used to show their prisoners. Their conversation was about the battles they had been in in Spain. Mr. Manuel and I were drinking some wine and listening to their conversation, while the landlady endeavoured through the means of a Swedish Officer lodged in her house to have us sent to another house. This officer in compliance to her wish went to the Bürgermeister's to have the bill changed, believing that we were French but when he understood we were Spaniards he not only brought back the bill but told the landlady to give me his own room as she had no other comfortable place in the house to put me in.

The French prisoners became gradually familiar until at last we entered into close conversation and learnt their whole story. They had been taken by Bernadotte at Leipzig and as many of them had served under him before his elevation to the throne of Sweden they were not only welcomed by him but even promised to be sent back to France.[43] For this purpose he caused them to follow the army instead of going to Siberia with the other French prisoners. To follow the movements of an Army as a prisoner is a very wretched thing even with the hopes of getting liberty. I saw it now in the impatience of these poor French, particularly in those who had been stript of all their property, that's to say, of all that they had plundered in Spain, for they had nothing else.

Mr. Peter was lodged in a house with a French Aide-de-Camp, a complete *muscadin du Palais Royal* [a coxcomb of the Palais Royal]. His manners were calculated to please ladies, and it appeared, at least by his conversation, that he had well succeeded with the Andalusian Ladies. When we spoke of Politics he inclined of course to the side of Napoleon, but as soon as he perceived that we would not agree with him, he gradually changed until at last he abused him as much as we had done. He did it very skillfully yet he did not escape our penetration, for when we feel a respective superiority above others we read their inmost thoughts in spite of their abilities.

Mr. Joseph was lodged with a passionate one with whom we had

43. Jean-Baptiste Bernadotte, one of Napoleon's marshals, was elected heir to the Swedish crown in 1810. He ruled as regent and crown prince before assuming the throne after the death of Charles XIII in 1818. In 1813 he broke with Napoleon and joined the allies against France, taking part in several key battles, including Leipzig.

like to have quarreled about politics, but a companion of his endeavoured to wave the subject, seeing that their situation was not the best for quarreling.

When I went home for supper the scene was completely changed—all was frankness, civility, and friendship between a Spaniard and two Swedes who were strangers to each other. The youngest of them was a fine lad and very well educated. He had already been a prisoner of the Russians, where he had been treated in the most horrid manner, for such is the hatred between these two nations, that the very Russians who behave most humanely to their French prisoners, behaved as barbarians to their Swedish ones. This enmity subsisted even after they were at peace, so much so that their Generals endeavoured to keep Swedish and Russian troops at a distance from each other for fear of disturbances. As a proof of this I was witness that these two officers, who had but a few soldiers, were obliged in the evening to conceal their uniforms with their cloaks when they went out, to prevent being insulted by a great party of Cossacks, which had entered the town by that time. These two officers seemed sincerely attached to the Crown Prince [Bernadotte], and they assured us that the whole nation was pleased with him. Undoubtedly he is a man who will make himself beloved by everybody; for besides the majesty and grace of his person, his affable yet dignified manners, which extended to all ranks must win every heart. He takes pleasure in shewing his munificence and humanity wherever he goes: for instance while he was at Cologne he supplied some hundred of Spaniards who were passing by that town with money.

The young Swede spoke to me of the organization of their troops. No man among them can aspire to the rank of an officer if he has not been educated in one of the military colleges. This gives to the Swedish Officers superiority in manners over the officers of other countries, among whom are to be found the man of education and the clown. Whatever advantage may be derived from this it is a real evil, for many uncultivated men display sometimes great military talents after a few campaigns in the rank of soldiers of which we have numberless instance in the French army.

The 5th March in the morning we set out for Cologne in the snow but as soon as we reached the plain we found a thaw, which always gives me an uncomfortable feeling. And who could feel otherwise in this mournful country?—an immense plain in which not a single mark of vegetation could be perceived?—mere lands as if just left by the floods?—when in those barren plains I feel as if I were going to sink into the main. I had always formed an idea of Cologne as a priest-ridden town, I do not know why, and now I was confirmed in my opinion when I saw the sterility and unpopulousness of the country, and more so when at a distance I descried the immense number of Churches belonging to that town. In my fit of ill humour I could not bear to remain in the carriage but walked by its side in the company of our Estevan, who with his usual fondness for conversation was puzzling me with questions about the topography, manners, and religion of the Country, and listening to my answers as if they came from an oracle. To say the truth, tho' he was one of the best informed of the Spanish soldiers, yet comparatively to his ignorance I might be called an oracle. Notwithstanding his ignorance, his mind and heart might be the pride of many a learned man. He could understand anything when explained in his own style, and feel anything provided the prejudices of his education were previously put aside by convincing him of their impropriety.

As we advanced we began to meet many small troops of peasants of both sexes with the appearance of people going to church or rather coming from some sanctuary, which still more corroborated my idea of the country being bigoted. I think Lady Montague [*sic*] gives it the same character.[44] What I can positively say is that I noticed an extreme similarity in this ecclesiastical appearance between Basel and Cologne. Ruminating on these thoughts I went on till I reached a small village where I bought some bread and spirits and where I discovered the

44. Lady Mary Wortley Montagu traveled across Europe in the early eighteenth century with her husband, Edward Wortley Montagu, who was sent on an embassy to Constantinople. *Letters Written during Her Travels* was published after her death.

vicinity to the Rhine by their receiving French coin in preference to the German. I stept into the carriage expecting every minute to reach Cologne. This town being so large we could not doubt but that the broadest road should lead us to it, so did not trouble ourselves about it. At last finding that we had gone a considerable distance without descrying the town we began to feel anxious. We found nobody of whom to inquire nor any crossroads to make trial of, so we went on. Soon afterwards we discovered the Town but in that very moment the road turned to the right and led us astray. We could no longer doubt we had taken the wrong way: we found a village a little further where we stopt to enquire our way and learned with great difficulty which was the crossroads from that place to Cologne. Three quarters of an hour after we were on the bank of the Rhine opposite Cologne. What a majestic river! Its sight was really awful from its size, its rapidity, and the enormous masses of ice floating down it. The vast town on the other side augments the grandeur of the sight.

My admiration for the beauty of the river was lost in anxiety about the difficulty of crossing it for I saw no public boats employed on this service nor did any boatman address us for that purpose. Notwithstanding, we took off the horses from our carriage when we were in the wharf and waited patiently until a boat came, on board of which we got without speaking a word. We ought not to have paid for our passage, being military men, but I so much longed to be on the other shore that I made no great difficulty in giving about the six shillings, the sum I was asked for our whole train. The wind was favourable so that in a few minutes we had crossed that part of the river which was not frozen but then came the ice, which tho' not completely congealed was yet a great impediment. In order to break it the boatmen made us stand and all together lean on one side of the boat and then on the other so as to rock it like a cradle, by which means we worked out our passage to the other bank. No sooner landed than we were assailed by a crowd of boys crying out to us *Ich vaise, ich vaise* (I know, I know), meaning thereby that every one of them could lead us to the place we wanted. In other circumstances it would have been an amusing spectacle to see the anxiety of these boys to gain the preference, to gain which they endeavoured to come as close to us as they could, which occasioned quarrels, pushes, and blows among themselves. I thought it expedient not to employ any of them but to make enquiries on our way. But there was no means of getting rid of these plagues. We were accompanied by most of them everywhere we went until I flew into a passion with the most troublesome one, swore at him in Spanish and gave him a blow instead of the sixpence he was expecting.

The town is large and handsome with many magnificent houses. Such large towns are always a curse to military men for besides the great distances we are obliged to walk there is always a complication of commandants, chiefs, and magistrates, extremely difficult to comprehend. The order of applications is peculiar to each town and if mistaken it produces great delays. After a long ramble through the town we found out the Platz-Commandant. His factotum was a young man 16 years old but very clever. He could speak German, French, Italian, and Latin, and when he found out that I could say some words in each of those languages he was so pleased that he showed me a particular friendship and attention in all the applications I had occasion to make to him. After all these steps were taken I went with Mr. Manuel to look for my lodgings. We had the good luck to frighten our poor Landlady, who out of fear, believing we were Cossacks, gave us immediately a good dinner, promised us a good supper and prepared two good beds for us. She was pleased to see her error when we told her we were not Cossacks.

Mr. Joseph was lodged in the same street in the house of a very rich Merchant. Every kind of attention was paid to him, and we were equally well treated as his visitors, when we called there. They had an English newspaper, which I was most agreeably surprised to find I understood.

It was night and the appointed hour to get our Marche-route, for which I was to call. I could not have it that night but in order not to lose the walk I had taken I looked for a Coffee House where I treated myself with my favourite beverage—punch. It was long before I could find a Coffee house for I saw nobody in the streets but women carrying baskets under their arms, who flew from me as I approached them to inquire for that place. I began to think I was in some fairy country. When I had enjoyed my punch I went home to enjoy my supper and then my bed. But pleasures cannot last forever—the morning came in. I was obliged to leave my delightful bed to go for the passport. What was worse than this was the news I got with the passport—that our coming to Cologne had been useless since we were to go to Dusseldorf on the other bank of the Rhine. The first thing therefore we had to do was to cross the river again and undergo of course all the troubles of the day before. Tho' I was glad I had seen this great town and proud to have seen with my own eyes the very shop of J. M. Farina happy distiller who made the only *veritable Eau de Cologne* for the Empress Maria Louisa, yet I could not bear the idea of twice crossing the Rhine in winter without any use to our main purpose.[45] In these thoughts I reached the wharf where I had the pleasure to see there was no ice in the river. We crossed it with favourable wind and without any expense for now I had learned I was not obliged to pay.

From Cologne to Dusseldorf we had two or three places marked in our passport in every one of which we thought we had a right to stop and exact rations but the first was opposite to Cologne in the other bank; the second half a mile further and the third was not upon the road. This second place had it not been in the neighbourhood of Cologne might have passed for a handsome and large town. The weather gradually became uncommonly cold. The road was fine but the country being flat presented no beauty. We were all of us out of humour[46] and spoke but little and then only to scold each other. The way seemed to us very long, and it was really so. When we had gone more than half of it without finding any village where we might eat

45. Jean-Marie Farina.

46. At the bottom of the page, there is an explanatory note: "this ['out of humour'] in English is far different from *ill humour*, the one being accidental, the other habitual."

our dinner we could not restrain our vexation. We were then told of an Inn a little further on. We dragged on to it and found it to be a comfortable one. Two *Diligences* from Dusseldorf had stopped there and the passengers, almost all Dutch as we perceived by their orange cockade, were eating a very good dinner. The comparison of their fine dresses and dinner with our own dress and the scanty dinner we were able to afford produced in us something of that feeling for which the English have composed a word borrowed from the French, *mauvaise-honte* [shame]. We had not courage to vanquish it and call for a poor dinner before those people, until at last I went to the kitchen and in my broken German I called for a soup and some meat I was told to wait until the table was disengaged. It was so very soon and we had a good dinner from the remains of the other. We paid not much for it.

The distance to Dusseldorf was rather long but as there was no place between in which we had a right to rations it became necessary to reach it that day. We went on as fast as we could. This part of the country is much finer than the preceding. We passed by an immense and beautiful country house or seat of a German Prince whose name I do not remember but I think I have been told it formerly belonged to the Bishop of Cologne. The country became more and more beautiful as we approached Dusseldorf but as the night approached in the same proportion we could not enjoy it. Yet I felt a kind of pleasure in seeing myself in a country, which had not the gloomy ecclesiastical appearance of Cologne. There was scarcely light enough to see the fine avenue leading to Dusseldorf when we reached this handsome town. Very luckily we met with a soldier of the militia of the country, who for the sake of being useful to old military men was good enough to lead us in the dark to all the places we wanted. As there were but few troops in the town we found everything easy.

We were sent all of us, servant and horses included, to a large house belonging to a Gentleman who during Bonaparte's power in the country had been employed in the *Droit-reunis* [tax collection]. His fortune and his belonging to Napoleon's system attracted him more severe charges. He was aware of it. While my companions went to the house I went with Estevan for the rations after which I went [blank][47] as I had already acquired the habit of drinking a glass of punch. When I had after long enquiry found a Coffee house I was nearly tempted to give up my project for it is impossible to imagine anything so dreadful as that alehouse. The smoke of the pipes was so thick that it might smother a person not accustomed to it. The noise of the conversation was very loud and the punch very bad. Nobody drank anything but beer out of glasses, which deserve commemoration for they were the oddest I ever saw. They were a high cylinder of glass large enough to contain a bottle of beer each. A whole party drank out of each of these cylinders.

I went home after my excursion and found my companions settled in two large rooms, waiting for the supper which we were to eat with the people of the house. I did not like it because we could not enjoy it freely; there was, however, an advantage in it, that we should be treated as well as the masters. The time came in which this was to be proved for we met with a nice and delicate supper and with great stiffness. Our Hosts were old and dry tho' polite. We endeavoured to look cheerful and we should have become so by drinking the good wine of our Host had it not been for the Hostess, who, knowing the too great fondness of her husband for wine, forbade any more to be brought. I noticed a singularity in the table—it was round and in its center there was another round, half the diameter of the table and two inches high. All the dishes were put upon this small round and as it turned on a pivot all the dishes passed in succession before the guests who helped themselves as they wished.[48] This contrivance is extremely convenient and has no other objection than for great joints if they are to be carved. After supper we went to bed. Each of us had a separate one, that's to say, a mattress on the floor with a few blankets.

47. "Where?" penned in below.

48. Comment at the bottom of the page: "I have seen this sort of table at Suppers where there was dancing and many to sit down."

The cold awoke us early in the morning but unfortunately we did not hurry our departure, thinking we should have plenty of time to reach Crevelt [Krefeld], which was only a few miles off. I spent more than an hour in hearing the two young boys of the house taking their lesson in violin. Neither of them could play on a regular sized violin, their hands not being big enough for it, but on their small one they plaid uncommonly well.

It was at least ten o'clock in the morning when we set out to cross the Rhine and pursue our journey. Our Landlord had made us out a sketch of the way after we had passed the water, with which we thought all the difficulties were over, but we soon saw our error when upon leaving the town we saw the Rhine all covered with ice but not hard enough to walk upon it. A few boats were carrying the people over but there were crowds waiting to pass and of course they had a right to go before us. Notwithstanding we did all in our power to get the preference: we ran from one place to another to see if we could get on some of the boats but all in vain.

We had already been more than two hours without being able to get into any boat, the extreme cold had chilled us and made us miserable, at the same time the ice hardened more and more and thus rendered the passage more and more difficult. All the people were equally impatient and now all order and restraint was lost, everyone attempted to get into the boats by force, and ourselves among the rest. In one of those attempts we had already nearly got our carriage on board when an officer of the Dutch militia who wanted to put his own carriage on board came and took off one of the boards upon which ours was placed and overturned it into the water. Mr. Manuel on account of his late illness had not stirred from the carriage during all this time and now we saw the moment in which he was going to be sunk into the river, but the boatmen and many other people exerted themselves so well that they prevented the carriage from being completely overturned and gave time to Mr. Manuel to get out. This scene turned out a most laughable one, for Mr. Peter who is not at all of a patient temper flew into a passion with the Dutchman and addressed him most bitterly in

Spanish: the Dutchman answered him in his own language, but Mr. Peter came up so close to him that tho' he did not understand Spanish he thought it expedient to be off and to retire. This eloquence of action procured us a more easy admittance and about one o'clock we were on board but men, horses, and carriages were crowded together in such a manner that the least motion endangered our being crushed or thrown into the water. To augment our inconveniences there was a stallion among the horses, an extremely fierce animal in Germany, for which reason almost all the horses there are [blank]. The man who brought it was obliged to remain next to him among the other horses in great danger of being crushed to death. The cold was now severer and yet we were obliged to remain in this state of misery for three quarters of an hour. The poor boatmen worked most dreadfully to break the ice but we were very often driven by the great masses of ice. It did not at all look like a navigation but rather as if we were dragged in a boat over land. About 2 o'clock we were safe on shore.

The greatest advantage I derived from getting on shore was the having it in my power to warm myself by walking but as it was dark we wanted to hurry and I could not have followed on foot. I sat therefore in the carriage with my sketch of the country in my hand comparing both as earnestly as a General commanding a great army could do. Tho' the sketch was very well done it was not guide enough for ascertaining when we arrived at any village whether it was the same we had in the map, and in the questions and answers we were often puzzled and fancied ourselves in the wrong road. The last time I thought myself so was upon entering a hilly and rather woody country where some waggoners told us that that was not the way to Krefeld. But I was in such a rage with all the difficulties of that day's journey that I swore I would make no more enquiries but go straight on until I found a Village. It was not very long before we did and there the question was to know whether we were to stop for dinner or not. It was late to stop but it was also late to do without a dinner; so we asked at the first house where we could find an inn. A girl of whom we enquired ran into her house without giving any answer but sent us a young man who to our great astonishment replied in Spanish to our question, saying, *Entre Vmds Caballeros* [Come in Gentlemen]. His house was an inn tho' there was no sign to prevent the intrusion of the soldiers who in time of war crowd those places, eat and drink without paying. In such a country, in such a village, and in such circumstance, who could have expected cleanliness and nicety in a public house? But in answer to this I shall say we were in Flanders, the rival of Holland in cleanliness without the affectation of the latter. Here, cleanliness is calculated to be enjoyed but in Holland it is only to be dreaded.

Our young man had paid very dear for his knowledge of the Spanish language for being with the French army against the gallant Mina had received a sabre wound, which divided his nose and the upper jaw so as to fall upon the lower and tho' the wound was now healed he could not masticate nor articulate distinctly.[49] This ill usage, however, did not at all make him averse to the Spaniards for he spoke with pleasure of the country and was as kind to us as if he had been our countryman or better. I can easily account for this apparent singularity, for having been torn from his family and country by Bonaparte he did not see in us those who had wounded him but those who had attempted to destroy those who had been the occasion of his wounds. We had a comfortable dinner for little money with the company of an assemblage of good natured, smiling country girls into the bargain. We were not very [far] from Krefeld: only a couple of hours journey. In about an hour we descried that place at the extremity of a vast plain like a spot on the horizon. We had no idea of what this town was, so that our astonishment was still greater. I never saw such an instance

49. There were two Minas to whom Fernando could be referring: Javier Mina Larrea, known as El Estudiante because of his studies at Saragossa when the War of Independence broke out, or his more famous uncle, Francisco Espoz y Mina, who took over his nephew's command of the Corso Terrestre de Navarra, a guerrilla band that operated in their native Navarre. The French captured Javier in 1810 and held him prisoner in the Vincennes fortress until 1814. In 1812 the Mina family was held hostage in France as a weapon against the guerrilla leaders. See the dossiers gathered in Archives Nationales de France, F7, 8775.

of neatness. All the houses seem new and are almost all uniform: there is no appearance of mud nor dust in the streets, quite as if never a horse or carriage had passed through them: in a word this town looks rather like one single building belonging to the corporation, the streets looking like the yards or courts belonging to it, than like any town.

We went to the Commune where we were received very politely by the Mayor's Secretary who after the usual complications told us he was ready to give us lodgings in the town, but they could not be such as were suitable to us for, said he, there had arrived the first detachment of Prussian troops and as that town had formerly belonged to Prussia and most likely would again come under their government the Mayor had expressed to them the satisfaction of the town by giving even to the common soldiers the lodgings usually given to officers. This satisfaction might easily be seen in every inhabitant's face and this is the case with all countries subjected to the Prussians—a most flattering proofs of their wisdom. Now for their sake we were obliged to go a few miles further to a village, the name of which I don't recollect, with an order to the Mayor to lodge us there. It was night when we arrived. The Mayor was a Grocer. His manners were not very polite but we spoke to him with a kind of authority, authorised by the written order we had. Mr. Manuel and I were lodged in an Ale-House and scarcely noticed by the landlord until we spoke to him with some animation and asked without compliment for a room, a fire, and a supper. When he saw our behaviour he called his son who could speak French to give us what we wanted. This young man, hearing us talk Spanish, fell into an error, which gave cause to a great deal of fun during our stay in the house—he imagined we were Russians and began to ask us many questions about Russia and the battles fought there. We saw that this error might be useful and agreeable so we let him remain in it. There was no battle in which we had not been, and of which we could not give an exact account, to which the young man listened with a kind of awe. Then we told him wonders about the climate and customs of our new country—Russia, every one of which augmented the respect and regards of the young man for us. Our supper was therefore a good one, and the attendance of the young man assiduous. In his absence we gave vent to our mirth with the natural pleasure in man of doing mischief. I think if there had been a good bed in the house it would have been for us, but tho' very bad the one we had was, I daresay, the best in the house.

I was chilled in it tho' with half my clothes on and with my companion beside me. The best way to be an early riser is to have an uncomfortable bed, we therefore rose next day before it was day. Our hosts were not awake and made us wait long before they gave us our coffee. This was the beginning of our sufferings of that day for it was one of the most severe winter days I ever have seen. A great deal of snow had fallen during the night and now the wind blew on our faces a kind of thick, icy fog which chilled our blood in our veins. The road was a cross one, and at the beginning was very difficult to pursue as it passed over woody mountains, the latter part of it was in a plain. This *givre* [frost] was so troublesome that we tried every means to preserve ourselves against it in our carriage but nothing would do, it penetrated notwithstanding the thick cloth we put before us and our clothes, whiskers and hair were covered with it. Poor Mr. Peter and Estevan who were without on the seat driving looked rather like balls of snow for this *givre* sticks to everything in all directions.

Very luckily the distance to Geldern where we were going was no more than four leagues, so at 12 o'clock we were in the town. Our disappointment would have been complete if in such a day we had been sent to some village beyond the town but as the Commandant was a young man of the town and a new soldier he exerted himself to shew every attention to old military men. He was the Captain of the Cossacks of the Country, for they have had the singularity of dressing and arming the militia just like Cossacks and of giving them this name. The Flemish Cossack was in his bed, for as this town is in the neighbourhood of the fortress of [blank][50] the troops of the country

50. Perhaps the French fortress at Wesel on the right bank of the Rhine.

were obliged to patrol all the night and sleep in the day. He wrote an order for the Commune to give us directly our due.

I was lodged in a fine house where I saw nothing but ladies. I endeavoured to appear as polite as possible because I was treated by them in the most polite manner. They were relations of the Mayor who from suspicions of having connections with the French had been sent to Cologne that very day to be judged: yet the poor ladies dared not complain. I dined with them: there was no meat because it was Lent and they were rigid observers of the practices of religion. They drank nothing but beer of a very thick kind that I did not dislike at all. This was the second time I began to like beer at my meals. I was asked to tea in the evening, which I missed, not caring then much about it. As we had arrived so early we knew not how to fill up our time. I spend the greatest part of the day and evening at Mr. Peter's playing the flute or minding the horses. We were rather uneasy about the mare, as since that valuable remedy of the veterinary Doctor of Frankfurt the poor animal had all one side sore. The remedy was rather cruel but its effects were desirable for she limped less and less in the proportion as we made use of it: and Mr. Peter who is a connoisseur in horses thought it good and kept it to take to Spain: thus by traveling is knowledge spread.

I spent some part of the day in ordering a silver clasp for my *carric* (French great coat) with which I was sure I should look as genteel again, and thereby get better lodgings on which depended all my happiness, and this was so powerful with me that, even the first months after I had been in England if anything went wrong I looked for consolation in the certainty of having after all a good bed and a good dinner. It is not to be wondered then, if the greater part of my journal speaks of nothing but the lodgings and meals. Another reason to excuse it is that the principal object in writing this journal was to retrace the different situations in which I have been during the whole journey, trifling as they may be, that in future I may perform it all over again in imagination.

I walked all about the town two or three times for it is small: and not handsome. In one of my excursions I met with a party of Spaniards, some of whom I knew, but as they were no friends of mine I saw no more of them. The tedium began so much to get the better of us in the evening that we had recourse to wine but in small quantity because it was very dear. I did not apply to my favorite punch because there was no coffee house in the town. The only thing they had like one was a kind of society of the gentlemen of the town to which nobody but themselves had a right to assist. Strangers who knew Gentlemen were admitted and under this denomination I was entitled to enter, but I could not bear the idea of asking for my punch without paying for it.

We had conceived the bold prospect of reaching Nimwegen [Nijmegen] next day by passing through Cleves [Kleve]; we were, consequently, to set out very early. Our Coffee retarded us a little yet we were on the road at dawn. I was in a melancholy mood and everything presented itself under disagreeable shapes: I almost fancied that we were to fall that day into the hands of our enemies, which was somewhat suggested by the knowledge I had of a powerful garrison of [blank] and the little confidence I had in the new soldiers besieging it. Had I not been absorbed in these wild fancies I should have enjoyed the aspect of the country, which tho' in winter was not at all disagreeable; the road being large and some pretty woods standing on both sides through which many pretty glades were seen. It continued so for about two or three leagues at which distance we found a village in which a regiment of Russian recruits was exercising not very skillfully. After we had passed this village the country is more barren and ugly. The road winds a great deal and the villages are shabby and poor. We stopped a moment in one of them where I eat some ginger bread and drank some gin, after which I began to be in better spirits. The Cossacks of this village and their awkward manner of performing their exercises pleased me beyond everything. We went on without any recurrence and about noon we were at Kleve.

The appearance of this town is very pleasant for being on a rising ground and having round it many pretty woods, parks, and avenues. We had been ascending a great deal until we came to the principal square in the town from which all the buildings before us were to be seen standing on such a steep that over the tops of the houses we could see the lower fields. The sun shone at that moment, which augmented the beauty of the prospect. The Prussians had the military command of the place and a handsome young officer of this nation, who was the Commandant, gave us everything we wanted with extreme politeness, for almost all the Prussians proved to be much of the gentlemen in their manners, at least with us. We wanted lodgings only to dine in, so we were sent to Inns. I went with Mr. Manuel to a fine one. The table was spread[51] for the ordinary, with which we were much pleased, thinking we were to partake of it. We asked if dinner would be soon ready but by the dry manner in which we were answered by the housekeeper we perceived she wanted us not to partake of such a good dinner. Besides that she was so much afraid that we should steal her plate that when she went out of the dining room she called one of the maids to watch us. Then she put dirty cloths and iron spoon and forks on a little table, where she served us a still dirtier dinner; yet as we had abundance we endured the rest patiently. The other gentlemen had better luck in their Inn, for they were admitted to the ordinary, at which we were present, having hurried out of our inhospitable inn as soon as we finished our dinner.

We had thought proper to sell our equipage before we arrived at the port in which we were to embark for fear of being obliged to give it for nothing. Here a Jew presented himself to buy it, and offered a good price, but Mr. Peter was dazzled with such a good outset and thought we might get a better price. I told him we should repent but [he] laught at me then, and next day acknowledged I was right.

We set out after dinner for the first town of Holland, Nijmegen. As this town is a considerable one and Kleve is of some importance I thought there was to be a high road between them but unaccountable as it may appear it is a fact that there is nothing that may be called a road leading from Kleve to Nijmegen. In descending the mountains

51. "*La table etoit mise*" penned in above.

of Kleve it looks rather like a ditch not wider than just to admit the carriage; at the bottom of the valley there is nothing more than the winding dykes of several canals and in ascending, which is the best part of it, there are some places in which the road is no wider than a pathway through a field. There is no village in the way nor passengers to whom we might apply for ascertaining if we were right, the night approaching apace therefore we began to feel uneasy. When we met any peasant we could not make ourselves understood not even with my broken German. Finally the night overtook us at some miles from Nijmegen and the road, which could scarcely be distinguished by daylight was now quite lost for us. The horses led us better than we could and stopped at the gates of the town when we thought ourselves many miles from it. A soldier of the guard conducted us to the Platz Commandant. I walked along with him noticing this odd town in which the houses may be said to have no front wall but a window taking the whole of the front of the house, from top to bottom at least in the tradesmen houses which composes the main part of the town. This in the night has a fine effect because the lights of the houses gives to them an air of illumination. A swarm of little boys followed me whispering in French "une jolie fille," [a pretty girl] "elle n'a que quinze ans," [she's only fifteen] "elle est charmante," [she is charming] and some added "elle est pucelle," [she is a maiden] which I doubted much. I met with a civil gentleman in the corps-de-garde who was going to do everything we asked of him, when the old cross Dutch Commandant entered and refused us everything. It was in vain we observed to him we wanted some rest after so many days traveling; he would not give us lodgings but for that night, and when we came to speak of the rations for our horses then, he burst into a passion with us and with the other Commanders who had granted them to us. They may do what they please, said he, but they have no authority upon me and I won't give a bit of straw for your horses nor carts to convey you. I cursed Holland with all my heart and complying with necessity we bought food for our horses, resolving to get rid of them as soon as possible.

I was lodged with Mr. Manuel in an Inn (which is called in Dutch *Logement*) of a good appearance. The people of the town and the passengers were all sitting in the parlour. We asked for our supper and room but no notice was taken of it. We then sat and began to curse Holland in our language. A young man, with the features of an East Indian, sitting by us perceived in our manners, when repeating the word *Holanda*, that we had some complaint against it and inquired about it in Dutch, to which as I did not understand it I asked him if he could speak French, no but I can speak English, said he in this language. I made an effort to answer him in the same and told him my complaints. He sympathised with me and assured me that everybody had to complain of the rudeness of the Commandant but that something might be said in his favour for really the town was overwhelmed with troops and recruits and there was scarcely room for them. This young man was born in Cape of Good Hope and had been many years a prisoner in England. He therefore sympathised with those who had been in that miserable state. He had no great complaints against the English nation but ascribed all his miseries to the dearness of the Country. He had just arrived with all the Dutch prisoners from England and nominated Ensign to the regiment under the command of our rude old officer. I had forgotten to say that when after all his refusals we asked him which was to be our further destination because our passport mentioned no other place beyond Nijmegen he answered he knew nothing at all, that some of our countrymen had gone to the Hague, some to Amsterdam, and some to Rotterdam. I could not bear this uncertainty nor the neglect of the Spanish and English governments of so many hundreds of their subjects and allies wandering all over Europe without finding any means to get home to fight, which was their most ardent wish. I now remembered half laughing and half in a passion the English Colonel's saying *mi tiene mucho barcos en la Haya para pasa Vm en Inglaterra* [Me have many boats in The Hague so that you can go in England]. Now the question was to resolve among ourselves where we should go. Mr. Peter among ourselves, who knew I was acquainted with a merchant of Amsterdam, proposed to go thither. I had no hopes of getting anything of him but in compliance to Mr. Peter I agreed to go to Amsterdam.

Let us now return to our inn and to the conversation of the Dutch African. He told me all the particulars necessary for the passage from Holland to England by the Packet, which discouraged me for I could not afford that expense. At a late hour came the supper at which we sat all together. It was good and I was hungry—nothing was wanted to prove that I relished it.

Our beds were not bad and we might enjoy them for we had resolved to remain in Nijmegen next day at our own expense since the Commandant would not give us lodging for more than that night.

I wrote before breakfast some letters and after breakfast we were going to leave the house to join our companions but were stopped by a maid who made us understand we should not go without paying. The landlady then came and said the same thing, but she could not or would not understand our answer. I asked for the gentleman who spoke English and told him how wrong that woman was in asking our reckoning since we were lodged in her house by the Commandant. That we were prisoners without any pay and supposed to be without a farthing of our own and consequently we had been everywhere fed in all our lodgings. He tried to answer my arguments but could not. He then spoke to another young man who had been also a prisoner with him and afterwards both spoke to the Landlady, who in a milder tone of voice told us we might go. I understood the generosity of the young Dutchmen but I had not been a Spaniard if I had suffered them to pay for me, so then I told them that I would not for the world put them to any expense for me: that I wanted only to ascertain whether I had a right or not to be fed, and that in case I were to pay I would do it with all my heart. I asked the Landlady to come with me to the Commandant but I was told she would be satisfied with a line from the said gentleman. We called on him and found him less rude than the day before. Our reasons convinced him, in consequence of which he sent a man to our landlady to assure her we were not to pay. The triumph of my *amour propre* was in its height when I entered the Inn with the man. The landlady looked rather sharp, the young officers looked pleased, and I more than all of them satisfied and thankful to them.

Upon leaving the inn we went to a Public house where our companions were employed in the sale of our equipage. The jockeys availed themselves of our situation to get it for nothing so after two hours bargaining it was settled that they should give us for the whole in French coins and take us in a coach to Tul [Tiel] next morning. As we had now money we agreed to pass that day in a good inn and get a good dinner. We went to the one in which Mr. Peter and his brother had been. There we spent a few hours in making ourselves clean. We made an exhibition of our persons in the principal square while we waited for dinner. We sat down to it and had a good one for little money, the wine excepted. It was the ordinary of the house so we had the company of many strangers, for which we did not care a bit.

After dinner we took a long walk round the town and had the opportunity to notice many things of which we were ignorant. The town is large and encompassed by fortified works, not very modern, and like almost all of those of Holland without lining [*sic*]. It was then unarmed. The main branch of the Rhine called there [Waal] passes by it, being there of a prodigious breadth.

In the evening we wanted to drink punch for which purpose we went about the streets looking for a Coffee house. We could not see anything in that shape but some houses on which was *Societait*. We ventured at last into one in which we learnt that this house belonged to a certain number of subscribers. The Dutch have a great number of these houses where they spend their time in drinking and smoking. We found with great difficulty a place to drink our punch in but it was very bad and we were surrounded by bad company, both of which took from me the illusion of this beverage. We went very wisely home without listening to the little boys, found our good supper and a better bed after it where we indulged til next morning.

Next day the 11th of March in the morning we got up early to endeavour to reach Utrecht. The Coach took us at our door and started at a good pace. It was of the kind called Dilligences in Holland. There is room for 6 inside and 3 outside but not on the roof as in England. There are no glasses but leather curtains so that when they are drawn the passengers remain in the dark without being able to see anything of the country. The way was over the dykes. It is most dangerous for these dykes are very elevated and narrow. An overturning here proves always fatal for on [one] side there is danger of being drowned and on the other of being shattered to pieces. There are very few places in which two coaches could pass together, therefore when at a distance two coaches descry each other, the one who arrives first to one of those places stops there until the other coach comes. The inns upon the dykes, and almost all the houses of the peasants in Holland look uncomfortable for they are paved with bricks upon which they throw water in great quantity many times a day to keep it clean. They merely brush away this water but do not drain it. Some throw on the ground some fine white sand. A kettle is always ready in those houses with coffee or tea, for they live upon these articles with cheese. The stables of the inns are parallel to the road and have two doors, by one the coach gets in and by the opposite it gets out. They are kept uncommonly clean. Nothing particular happened to us during our way to Tiel, I only employed myself in comprehending the plan upon which those dykes are built, to keep the waters from the low plains, which are beneath the level of the sea, and in admiring of their solidity. It was impossible to judge of the beauty produced by this combination of plain, river, and canals, for now all were in their winter sleep, but in summer when all conveyances are made by water and the plains covered with every production, nothing, I daresay, can be pleasanter than a walk upon the dykes. Even the boats and vessels are an ornament to the scene, for this nation living always upon the water have carried there luxury and nicety. The meanest of all the boats for carrying bricks is handsomely painted like pleasure boats. As to the larger vessels employed in the navigation of the Rhine, they are extremely fine.

About noon we were opposite to Tiel. The coach was not to carry us any further. We stept out of it and saw before us the river larger than we had ever seen it and quite frozen. People and carts were crossing it as quietly as if they were walking on shore. The perpetual passing had made a path on the ice so as to make it look like a road. I walked with confidence yet it could not but tickle me the idea of being upon such a river supported only by a few inches of ice. It took me a quarter of an hour to cross it, and I was not sorry when I was on shore. The ice had been broken near that bank but they had put a kind of draw-bridge from shore to the ice and it stood perfectly well. What looked to me most unaccountable was that a little lower down the river was not frozen at all.

With sunshine and great spirits we entered Tiel, a pretty little town. The Platz Commandant was in a Societat drinking gin and smoking. He gave us very politely what we wanted. Upon presenting his order to the Commune, which by the bye was a handsome building, we had the tickets for our dinner and the promise of carts against 2 o'clock. In the Logement in which I was the ordinary was not ready, so they hurried some of their dishes and gave us a good dinner with a bottle of good wine. This wine, which usually they drink in Holland must come I think from the hills along the Rhine in Germany, for it has the same peculiar taste with this and that of Neuchâtel. It tastes a great deal of the branch of the vine. It gave me always the idea of not being made of grapes but of raisins, yet when good I liked it much.

The people of the Logement were so attentive that I went to the kitchen before we left the house to thank the Landlady. The good fat Dutch woman made me a thousand excuses for the dinner not being well done but if we wished to stay a little longer she was preparing something better. I really felt most thankful for her goodness, and went to the appointed place for the carts. They were not punctual, so that we might not wait in the streets we entered a coffee house, where I drank for the first time a good gin, if it was gin which I drank. There are two sorts, one white and the other reddish, the latter being rather sour.

The carts came at last and tho' not commodious we were happy to have them. Their shape was very odd. They are long and narrow. The bottom shelves from the hind part to the foremost and in the same direction it diminishes in breadth. Of course all this part being on the axle-tree the motion is most unpleasant, particularly over the paved roads, of which there are many in Holland. We were now traveling inland, and noticing a peculiarity of the roads—that their turns are all in right angles and none in curves. We got on quick enough, passed by a small town and soon arrived at a village where we were to have other carts. The garrison was composed of a few Prussian soldiers, one of whom conceived so high a respect for us that he set all the village in motion to procure us our carts without delay: helpt us out of ours, shewed us into a house to wait for the fresh ones, and with many bows assisted us to mount them. We went in these a few miles further along many pretty canals. On the banks of one of these was the house of the Mayor who was to give us fresh carts. He was an ill-tempered clown, tho' polite. His house was dark and black but clean: with a little chimney, a fire, a very rare thing in the country for they make use only of stoves. We set off [52] near dark in carts not so good as the preceding ones.

I do not remember if it was this part of the road or the former that we crossed two broad branches of the Rhine at a little distance from each other. We did not move from our carts to cross them, for the boats are so convenient that any carriage goes in with great ease. We crossed the first with rowing, but the second was frozen in its upper part so that the boatmen towed us walking over the ice. It was quite dark when we reached the place where our carts were to be changed. The men told us to get out of them to which we answered that we would when they procured us the others. A great number of the inhabitants had surrounded us among which was the Mayor, as we inferred by the cartmen applying to him for carts. He looked very sullen and answered he had none to dispose of. The elder of these cartmen was a passionate man and his temper occasioned a very laughable scene between him and ourselves, for when he saw we would not stir from

52. Parenthetical comment: "*advierte que* set *es preterito y participio de* to set (note that *set* is preterit and participle of *to set*)."

the carts he turned back the way he had come, hurrying his horses. Mr. Peter who was next to him caught him by the arms, pushing him backwards to catch hold of the reins; he struggled against Mr. Peter and whipped his horses in a rage. Then I came nearer to help Mr. Peter, while Estevan, who was out of the cart took the horses by the bridle and stopped them. Our victory over the stubborn fellow was signalised by the loud acclamations and laughter of the multitude. The poor devil yielded to force and went on to Utrecht. He became gradually tractable and good natured and at last humbly begged we would not oblige him to go into the town for fear they should detain him for next day. His petition being reasonable was granted, whereby we shewed our generosity for we were obliged to walk a long way loaded with our luggage.

Utrecht is a large and handsome town in the peculiar style of the Dutch towns, with a large canal through the middle of every street, or, in more correct terms, there are no streets but rather wharfs belonging to the canals on which the houses are built. This must give great cheerfulness to the towns in summer but at the same time it gives a great monotony to them. In Amsterdam it is so much so that all the streets looked to me the same and I could hardly distinguish one from another. We were at great pains to get our lodgings at Utrecht. Nobody could inform us of the Platz Commandant until we met with a boy who undertook to conduct us there. He took us to the Dutch commandant whose powers were much circumscribed by there being a Prussian garrison in the town. Nobody therefore applied to him, and consequently our application was most flattering to him. The poor old man and his family rivaled each other in politeness towards us, but when he came to tell us that we must apply to the Prussian Commandant for the carts because they were not at his command we were rather vexed, tho' we looked civil in return for his good wishes.

We had now to walk a great way to the Prussian Commander, who was lodged in one of the principal houses of the town. With his orders we were obliged to walk to the mansion for lodging and to another place rather distant for the carts for next day. Already knocked up with fatigue and cold Mr. Manuel and I reached our lodgings. The house looked handsome, the hall and corridors were paved with white and blue marbles like most of the Dutch houses. This looks very neat but it is so cold that it makes one chilly only to look at the floor.

With all this neatness in the exterior, the inner part of the house was rather shabby. An old man and his wife with a daughter, rather elderly, were sitting round a stove. We sat by them expecting with eagerness the supper. It was long before it came and all this time was passed in conversation between my friend and me for our hosts could speak nothing but Dutch. When supper was ready the son of the family entered and conversed with us. The supper was rather scanty except in the article of cheese for these people live chiefly upon it. The landlord was a lawyer and had a large library at the bottom of which there was an alcove with our bed. The room was exceedingly cold and the bed hard yet it was late when we awoke next morning. We hurried our breakfast and went for the Carts; but what was our astonishment when we saw the two friends Sierra and Clausel getting into a Cart! These two fellows like many other of the Spanish officers who had entered into the French service during Napoleon's glories had forsaken him now and wanted to go back to Spain.[53] I had been acquainted with them but their behaviour had alienated me so much from them that I did not speak a word to them. Mr. Manuel was not so particular and went up to them. Their story was an incomprehensible one for first of all they were going the same way we had come, and then they said they were coming from the Hague because they could not find there any ship for England. We parted and we have heard nothing of them since.

Amsterdam was our destination, the place in which my hopes were fixed as well as those of my companions. In our way for it we had many

53. Depending on their rank, these men might soon have been banned from returning home. Ferdinand VII's May 30, 1814, decree prohibited the return of army officers from the rank of captain and above who had served Joseph I. See Juan López Tobar, *Los famosos traidores: Los afrancesados durante la crisis del Antiguo Régimen (1808–1833)* (Madrid: Biblioteca Nueva, 2001), 114–24.

things to for the[54] country is much varied at least comparatively for the monotony of Holland. At first the country was barren but afterwards ensued a section of country villas of great variety and magnificence all surrounded and intersected by pretty canals communicating with the road by drawbridges and the latter part of this journey[55] was all in canals, orchards and gardens. Several handsome villages lay in the way. The road is narrow but not so much as that over the Dykes. Some parts of it were like the usual roads, some parts paved with flint and some in a very excellent way and peculiar to Holland this is to pave with bricks united to each other by the flat part and presenting only the edges. It is exactly the manner in which many of our vestibules at Seville are paved. The Carriages having the *yantas* [*llantas*—the rims of the wheels][56] quite flat render this kind of road extremely smooth to such a degree that the motion of our carts without springs was very gentle. Quite the reverse happens in the other roads paved with flint for nothing can be so dreadful as the motion of those carts. I could scarcely bear it. All along the road and in the villages we saw marks of the rejoicings which took place after that country was freed from the tyranny of Napoleon. For the same reason every man in Holland wore the orange colour ribbon.

When we reached the first village on our way, our driver went to the Mayor to be relieved, and I then noticed two singularities of this country: one, that the country people when they enter a house leave their shoes at the door and walk with nothing but their stockings over the stone pavement without the least sign of feeling the cold; and the other is that in the offices nobody sits to write but they stand, their desks being made for that purpose higher than in other countries. We

54. Footnote in diary: "Something is wanting here to make sense of the passage."

55. Footnote in diary: "This is by no means *English* and I have been obliged to *interpolate* in order to connect the sense, tho' I perfectly well know what you mean."

CSN: The corrections are: "the latter part of this journey" replacing "and the last part," and "lay in the" replacing "were found that."

56. Note beneath word: "no such word in Newman's dictionary."

could not get our carts exchanged, and we felt for our poor driver, who was a good man. To have him pleased we took him to breakfast with us, our breakfast being composed of bread, butter, and cheese with gin and brandy. We pursued our journey to the next village, hoping we could have there our cartman relieved, but we were disappointed also. A blacksmith, who was the most respectable person of the village and without doubt the most impudent came to us and said he had nothing to do with our business, that we might go to the neighbouring place if we wanted carts for there were none in that village. To this we paid no attention but inquired after the Mayor, to which he and a crowd of women and children answered unanimously the Mayor was too much engaged and could see nobody. When we saw this obstinacy we went back to our carts and pursued our journey. We reached very soon the next village in which we saw many handsome houses. The finest was that of the Mayor. When our cartman had called there a young gentleman most elegantly drest came to us and in very good French told us to go to the Inn, where he would send immediately carts. We saw him exerting himself to get them ready. Meanwhile, we were entertained in seeing a troop of recruits and women conducted by an old soldier quite tipsy as well as the women and recruits.

Finally the carts came and after two hours of the most dreadful jolting we arrived at the magnificent town of Amsterdam. This town was commanded by the troops of the country. A great part of the officers being newly made, had not yet acquired the rudeness of old soldiers, therefore they were very civil and obliging. As the town is very large we had a great deal to walk, first to the General then to the Platz-Commandant and afterwards to the *Commune*. In one of these places we met our long lost, but not regretted, Brotons. He had not changed his manners, and with his flattery attained everything. Here he was dispatched the first, and we were not sorry for it, for we longed to see him far from us. It was not without difficulty that we obtained three days rest in that town; yet it was granted when I said that my object was to take some money to continue my journey.

At the Commune I got the direction of my late bankers, Messers Willink et D'arripe but without hopes of getting anything of them.[57]

We separately lodged but near one another. I was in a Tanner's house, but it looked like a gentleman's house, and so are almost all the tradesmen houses for the shops have very little appearance. The great difference is in the cleanness, for the tradesmen houses cannot be kept so nicely as the others. The family of my house was composed of a young married man, his wife and her sister: all of them very good-natured and obliging. The sister could show it better for she could speak French very fluently and had a pleasure in speaking it and reading it, as I knew afterwards because she was in love with a French sergeant. Poor soul, she had lost him perhaps forever, yet she felt a delight in speaking that language which had conveyed to her heart the feelings of her lover. Oh! happy shalt I call me if my conversation could console that poor broken heart. I knew not then

57. According to diplomatic correspondence, Spain's minister to Amsterdam and the consul general had left their archives with José d'Arripe when they were forced to flee the country in 1808 because of their refusal to swear the oath of loyalty to Joseph Bonaparte. In their correspondence of 1813 and 1814, informing the government of these actions and testifying to d'Arripe's trustworthiness, they praised him for the help that he gave to the Spanish prisoners as they passed through the city. D'Arripe, according to the former consul general, Bias de Mendizabal, was a Bearnese who had spent his youth in Santander, and thus "has always wanted to consider himself, and has always been considered Spanish both in Spain and in Holland, where he accordingly was given a Spanish passport whenever he traveled during my consulship in that country, and his firm [Casa de Comercio] was always considered in that place as a Spanish house because of his sentiments and because of his many relations with Spain." See Dn. Bias de Mendizabal to Excmo. Sr. Encargado de la Sec.a del Desp.o de Estado. En contestatión a su Oficio de 6 del corriente dice quien es Dn. José d'Arripe de Amsterdam, y porque quedaron en su poder los Archivos del Ministro del Rey y del Consulado Español en Holanda, dated Tangiers, February 28, 1814, AHN/E, legajo 6006/1, no. 14. The lesson to draw, and which is confirmed by Fernando's experience, is that having no relations since 1808 with countries controlled by France, the restored Spanish government was in no position to offer assistance to the thousands of Spanish prisoners flowing through the Netherlands.

to appreciate her sufferings. Perhaps I would have laught at them—but not now.

I made myself a little clean and went to look for the house of Messers Willink and D'arripe. It was not an easy matter in such a town without knowing the language. I shewed the direction to many persons but their explanation was lost for me. At last I found it but new difficulties arose, for the servants did not understand me, nor would let me in because they feared I would dirty the house. Owing to my obstinacy I obtained that a maid went for her Mistress to let her know the great danger in which the house was to be dirtied by a stubborn soldier. The Lady had better come herself to the door to speak to me than let me in with my muddy shoes. When I saw her I was going to approach but she hastened her pace towards me looking at my feet with great anxiety, that I should not pass the threshold. I told her my case and my connections with her husband, to which she replied that he was not the Willink partner of D'arripe but his brother and that this had been ruined by his partner, yet I might call in the evening if I want to speak to her husband. After all this I lost all hopes of getting anything, yet I made up my mind not to desist from my purpose for want of patience, but to endure all these humiliations with philosophy.

After this resolution I went home for my dinner, which in that moment I did really want more than any money in the world. My good people had prepared me the best they could afford with half a bottle of wine, which made me forget the humiliations and the appointment.

I was at Mr. Willink's a few minutes after the time, and was told that he had not been able to stay any longer, but I might call next day. Before I came home I tryed and looked for the house of the real Willink. I found it but the reception here was more rude. A very pretty boy was my interpreter, perhaps Mr. W's son. I gave up this scheme resolved, however, to pursue the other. In going home in thought of drinking a glass of punch, I entered a Coffee house which was deserted and where I had very bad punch. I went home to get my supper and bed.

In my excursions I had had opportunity to notice the neatness of the most mean shops; the beauty of the principal square in which is the magnificent Palace of the late King; and the peculiar construction of the rich houses. The first floor is only 6 or 7 feet over the level of the ground. Beneath this floor is that part of the English houses which in England is under the level of the streets, that is to say the kitchen and rooms for servants etc. The entrance to this part of the house, which also leads to the counting houses, by a door over which there are two stairs forming an arc close to the wall and leading to the principal door of the first floor, but by this door nobody goes but visitors.

Next day being a Sunday and having to wait upon my merchant I was extremely particular in my *toilette* yet dirty enough to frighten all the maids of a Dutch house. I called in all my finery at Mr. W.'s but he had gone to church. I walked sometime along the streets and called again. He was not yet come. Then I walked before the door and called again. The servant pitied me and showed me into a Parlour all covered with gild paper of the most ancient taste, but very neat. I began to grow tired of waiting when one of the maids singing a French air gave me an idea of killing the time. My flute was always in my pocket so I took it out and began to play the same air with the maid. She began another, which I accompanied too, then I plaid to myself and passed the time. I do not know if it was the power of melody or if it is the custom of the country the maid came with a cup of coffee and a small cake, which she offered me very politely, but my pride did not me allow to accept of it.

At last Mr. Willink arrived with his brother, my correspondent, both of them of a very genteel appearance and tho' not old yet dressed much in the old fashion. The first addressed me and told me all the misfortunes of his brother, and that the house had been dissolved, Mr. D'arripe having been obliged to fly to England because he had been compromised with the French government for having connections with that Country. My usual pride was going to spoil everything for I answered to this I was sorry I had disturbed them and begged their pardon. Yet Sir, added he, if we can be of any use for you it will be with great pleasure. Then I resumed courage and said I was in distress and if they trusted me I would draw for a small sum on Messers J. Lubbock and co. It was immediately granted, they only differed in the quantity for they did not choose to make any considerable advance. They gave me about twelve pounds for which I felt most thankful. Here I had the first tidings of my friend and townsman [Antonio Maria] Oviedo, since he had made his escape a year before from Besançon. Mr. Willink had heard from him during his stay at Trieste.

Nothing but the pleasures of a tender passion can, I think, be superior to that of having money after some time's distress. This was the third time I was in this case, yet it put me nearly out of my senses when I felt my pockets full of crowns. My head ached a little for which reason I entered a coffee house to drink a cup of coffee. It was one o'clock and the house was full of people drinking coffee and chocolate, an odd custom indeed. After this I went to my companions to give them the good news at which they rejoiced very much, and that there should be some festival upon the occasion I engaged them all to drink punch in the evening, and left them to go to dinner. We met in the afternoon and walked about for our pleasure and for our business because we intended to set off next day since my purpose had been fulfilled.

Already in the morning those Gentlemen had been doing a great deal about this matter from which I had been generally freed by them on account of my appointment at Mr. Willink's. The great object was to get carts to Rotterdam upon which a very laughable thing took place between Mr. Peter and the Platz Commandant. The latter said he could not give us carts: why replied Mr. Peter, are there not *Diligences* in this country?—Will you go by the *Diligence*, said the Commandant?—To be sure we will, answered Mr. P.—Well then I'll give an order for your places in it.—When we knew this we could but laugh to see a man who refused carts and gave a far better and far [more] expensive thing.

We spent the evening in the Coffee house after which we began to think of changing my money for it was all in silver and very burthensome therefore. We could not find any gold, until at last in the house of Mr. Manuel we met a very obliging young gentleman, very fond of everything English, said he, because his father was an Englishman and was sure his father would do anything for me only because my name was White. This gentleman was an Innkeeper who gave me as a great favour some gold coins of all nations, among which two half guineas. I did not know the value of the money but he made a hasty calculation in which I am sure he was not a loser.

I went home not for supper, for I had been told that we would not have any but to drink chocolate. This had been proposed to me as a dainty. I therefore expected some good thing. I waited till midnight at which time they came from a family Comedy and began their chocolate. They put a kettle with milk on the fire and when it boiled they put the chocolate within but in so little quantity that the milk had scarcely lost its colour: yet in proportion we drank they poured milk in the kettle. We eat with this beverage slices of bread between two of which there were slices of cheese and of cold meat. I do not know how many cups we drank for the Dutch are never satisfied of drinking these things; which gave occasion to my saying, and past afterwards among us as a proverb, that the Dutch were so fond of canals that even within their bodies they wanted to establish them. Ever since, instead of saying I am going to drink tea or Coffee we said I am going to establish the Canals.

With my stomach full of hot milk and my purse full of money I went to bed the happiest man alive. My bed was in an alcove near to the drawing room, which I so well remember that I could give a drawing of it. Its furniture as well as that of the houses of my companions had a great similarity with the old fashioned furniture of my country; and I think it very easy to account for it: for the fashions of the Lower Countries were brought to Spain in the times we were Masters there, and now they are existing only in old houses in Spain and in the houses of the poor in Holland, where they had their origin. I said poor and I was wrong in calling so our Landlords. They may be styled so comparatively with the classes of Merchants and the *proprietaires* but in general I have seen very few people in Holland that might be called poor. This Country must have been far superior to England in the times of its prosperity but England has greater treasures independent of riches. The English women are infinitely handsomer than the Dutch; nay, the very comparison injures these lovely charmers, for there is no Dutch woman that I have seen who might be said tolerably pretty. Let us then hasten to England, this happy country blessed by Heaven with riches, power, and beauty. But they shall be mine, or shall I only be the wretched and covetous spectator of the bliss of these proud islanders?

I must not smother the high spirits in which the mere recollection of my happy mood in the 14th March 1814 puts me, with an untimed prevision. Perseverance perhaps will make all that mine. What will not time do? Time freed me of my chains, time brought me to England, time—but how can I enumerate everything? Time will end this journal if I am not always so talkative and chattering out of purpose as I am now.

Not wiser than I am now but for different motives I left Amsterdam and my good landlords early in the morning on the 14th. We had a Diligence like those I have already described out of which nothing can be seen, but I did not care for it that day for I had within myself a sufficient store of happiness. Our drivers were very fond of stopping at all the Inns, and as I was in so high spirits that day I followed their example, and drank coffee, gin and brandy ten or twelve times in the day. The weather was very proper for that strain of life for it was very cold. We stopped for dinner in a village together with the passengers of another Diligence. We were all merry before dinner, so afterwards we were fools; we abused the Dutch, tormented the maids, and made as much noise as a party of French *Compagnons* (I knew a great deal of this corporation and our Estevan, who was in it told me more: perhaps *par la suite* I'll give an account of it) going to do *le devoir* to some of their fellows.[58] We passed in our way many villages and some towns but as we were buried alive in our Diligence we did not see anything else but the Inn or the Coffee house.

We arrived at Rotterdam in the night, and alighted at a public

58. The *compagnons de devoir* were youths apprenticed in skilled trades who perfected their craft by making the Tour de France.

house, but not thinking it proper for a possessor of twelve guineas we went to look for a Logement. A poor young woman for a little money shewed us to a good one, very much in the style of the English hotels. As soon as we entered the parlour the servants came to pull off our boots and give us slippers for such is the nicety of these people that even in an hotel it is not allowed to remain with dirty boots. We had a fire like in England, the supper was much in the English manner, all which together with their being Englishmen made me suspect that this hotel was much resorted by English travelers. We had beefsteaks besides a few other dishes, but what I liked the best there as well in all other parts of Holland is the potatoes and the melted butter for them. The potatoes are much better than the English, and they know so well how to melt the butter without making it oily that I will always prefer it to the English butter sauce.

Our conversation during supper was about our journey and upon this occasion we observed how proud we should be when talking in Spain among our countrymen who had not stirred from their homes, we should name those pompous names of Amsterdam, Rotterdam, Frankfurt, Karlsruhe, London, etc. Our happy mood was not altered during the whole day. We went to bed in the same mood. Our beds were good and clean so we had nothing to wish. We had not thought of taking military lodgings, first because we could afford a better lodging with our own money, but next day we intended to present ourselves to military Commanders of the town to get lodgings and remain there till the other day.

We ate our breakfast, in which we had a kind of biscuit which open very easily by the middle and are very good with butter, and afterwards we went to the Commandant's where we were told to apply to the Spanish Consul. In his house we were shown by a maid into a storehouse full of butts of wine and brandy at the end of which there was an Office in which the Consul was writing. I addressed him in Spanish but he answered me in French he did not understand that language. It must be acknowledged that he had not been very well chosen for that place. If this choice surprised me I was much more so when I read the correspondence between him and the Spanish Ambassador in England. The Consul had exerted himself as much as possible to get means of relieving the numberless officers and soldiers daily applying to him in the greatest distress, but the Ambassador answered he had nothing to give.[59] We enquired if it had been provided for our embarquement and were answered there was at Hellevoetsluis an English Captain King who was charged of it. The Consul gave us a bit of paper with the name of the Captain, our own and our respective rank and signed it. We kept this paper with great care, thinking it was a positive order for our embarquement.

We took leave of the Consul and went for our lodgings, but the Commandant said we could very well go to Hellevoetsluis that day: we objected the want of conveyance. You will have carts, answered he: so there was no manner of opposing. We went home and prepared with sorrow for our departure as if we had a foreboding of what expected us in the night. In our running about for our business we saw a great part of Rotterdam. I think it is handsomer than Amsterdam and cleaner. The canals are broader and the ships bigger and better looking.

We were not quite ready when the Diligence was at our door. I entered it with as gloomy a turn of mind as it had been lively the day before. The little I could see of the road and country increased my melancholy. We arrived at a village where we ought to have another conveyance for which we waited in a public house. I was not hungry but we asked some bread, butter, and cheese and I began to eat it but in that moment I began to feel the effects of the steam of boiling tar, which they had in the middle of the room. It made me quite sick without being aware of the cause. My uncomfortable feeling made me cross and gave occasion to my companions' jokes. When the cart

59. This was apparently Anton F. van Schelle. See his note to Count Fernán-Núñez enclosed in dispatch no. 379, dated London, February 24, 1814, AHN/E, legajo 5466. In the same dispatch, Fernán-Núñez reported the arrival of eight Spanish officers escaped from France, including the captain of infantry, Rafael de Riego, soon to take on a major role in the struggle between absolutism and liberalism in Spain.

came and that I went out of that previous room I began to feel well; by which I came to know the cause of my illness. There was no road but the dykes which was so rugged by the mud being frost that the jolting of the cart almost broke our bones. After a few miles jolting we met a village from which the cartman wanted to go but we stopped him until we had another. We applied to the Mayor who answered that no carts were given in that place because there was a large river [Maas/Meuse] to pass: that on the other side we find conveyance for Brielle. The cartman and the people of the village were angry because we had detained him, and now expressed this triumph with great contentment.

As we arrived at the place of embarquement we saw a broad river and a nice little boat sailing towards us. The wind was high and contrary to come to our shore, so we expected long before it arrived. We went on board with such a quantity of people that there was no room left for the sailors to move. Luckily the wind was fair and in a few minutes we crossed. Here was a kind of Inn where the carts were to be given to us but when we said we ought not to pay for them they said they had none. We asked for the Mayor, to whom we applied for redress but he proved to be the most stubborn and ill-natured clown of the Country. Nothing could be obtained and as there were but a few miles to Brielle I prevailed upon my companions to walk thither.

It was quite night when we arrived within sight of Brielle, and now too lately we were in an Island almost desert without means of passing to Brielle for the boats had remained in the other side, the wind not being fair to come to our shore. When we arrived opposite to Brielle we found a kind of public house, or else an alehouse for the mariners. The people of the house, tho' they had no hopes that the boat would come, hoisted a lamp for more than half an hour to make sign to the boatman that there were passengers on this side: All was useless and the only prospect we had was to remain in that alehouse, but what was our astonishment when we saw a decided opposition from the people of it. We prayed, we menaced, we showed our money that they might not be unconfident but all in vain. No, no, no, was their only answer.

They were so anxious to get rid of us that they proposed to take us in a cart to the Mayor's to get lodgings. We were obliged to accept of it and so by a most cold and dark night and half starved we undertook our journey to the Mayor's. We took also with us, out of pity, a Spanish soldier who was in the alehouse before us almost naked and starved. It took us near an hour to go to the Mayor's during which time we were much tormented by hunger and cold. Our cartman introduced us to the Mayor in the stable where he was milking his cows. After a long conversation between the Mayor, cartman, and Mairess [*sic*] we had some bits of paper instead of tickets for lodgings. We thought we were to remain in the neighborhood of the Mayor but our desperation was unutterable when we understood that we had to go to the part where we came from and on foot because, they said, the horses were ill. It really seemed made on purpose by Providence to show us how little man ought to put his confidence in money: for the first day we had had money in plenty we could not find with it the least comfort: even Dutch innkeepers would refuse it, a thing really which I never could account for.

The cartman showed us the way back without which I am sure we would have never made it out but how miserable we were now! Exhausted with fatigue and hunger, numb with cold and our feet almost rent with the ruggedness of the ground. Notwithstanding all our misery we felt a secret pleasure when upon arriving at the alehouse from where we were sent off we saw the Cartman giving the ticket to the landlord. Now said we he must have us for nothing after he has refused to take us by paying. But this was the night of the disappointments for he read the ticket and pointed somewhere in the fields. We asked to be conducted where it was, and he ordered a boy with a lamp to shew us the way. This boy and a lad took us to the path leading to the farm where we were to be lodged but would not go as far as that. Then I lost all patience and restraint, caught hold of the boy's arm and swore to him in Spanish in the most violent manner he should show us the way. The poor boy trembled to see me in such a fit of passion, the lad laughed at the boy's dread, and both yielded and conducted us to the farm, which surely we had never found without them. We gave them some money tho' they did not deserve it for their stubbornness. The farm appeared to us a Palace after all the fatigues of that day. It was better than anything we had seen in the Island, for cleanness and comforts tho' in general the houses of the Dutch peasants do not abound with them. Their fires are so scanty that anybody but them would be chilled.

The one we had now was not so, for we could keep ourselves warm near it. We expressed to our fat farmer, who was sitting by the fire without shoes, that we had not eaten any dinner and were very hungry; in consequence of which he ordered his wife and daughters, who were waiting on him as *slaves*, to give us something. But who that knows not Holland could have imagined what this woman thought proper to give to people who by eleven in the night had eaten no dinner? She gave us *tea*. The canals came immediately to our recollection, and in spite of our hunger and fatigue we had much fun about it. We ate with our tea some slices of bread and butter with slices of cheese between them. If this dinner was not sufficient at least it had the effect of warming me, which I wanted much. We had two clean but hard beds for us four in the upper part of the cottage, which I must not call first floor for it was nothing but the space between the two declivities of the roof, so from our beds we could touch the roof.

We slept until late the next morning when Estevan and the poor soldier, who had remained in a farm near the Mayor's, came to wake us. We dressed and ate a breakfast equal to the supper, shook our good farmer by the hand and went to the place of embarquement. The sight of Brielle gave us hopes of being there well for it was not a small town, but the boat had just gone to the other side and we must expect a long while before it came back. We waited with great anxiety for nearly two hours. Already we began to think that perhaps the ice of the other side was too thick, for the boat to go through and feared it to be confined in the Island.

The boat came at last and we landed with great pleasure at Brielle thinking all our pains over, but we began to see great numbers of

Spaniards, easily known by their features, which tempted our curiosity.[60] We approached one of them to ask them what they were doing there. Sir, said he, we are here a few hundreds of soldiers and many officers waiting for transports to go to England. We did not like at all this intelligence yet as we had the paper from the Consul we hoped this did not regard us. But soon we met with many officers of our acquaintance from whom we learned that the paper was of no use. We learned everything as follows. All the Spaniards coming by Holland were sent to that town to wait for transports. The soldiers were in barracks, and so were the Officers but in better ones. The letter had an allowance of one pound meat, one pound and a half bread, with some vegetables and salt, and a bottle of wine and a third part of a bottle of gin, to which it was added 20 turfs for cooking and warming. This account without seeing the things was very favourable to us, the uncertainty of our embarkment excepted and the necessity of living with a great number of people we disliked. When we saw these things nothing but the number of friends we had there could make us bear them with patience. The house in which the greatest part of the officers were was that of the Prefect, which when the Dutch shaked off

60. Early in 1814, the Spanish minister in London, Fernán-Núñez, reported to his government that the restored Dutch sovereign, the Prince of Orange, ordered the concentration of 1,500 Spanish escapees and deserters in Brielle, where they would await embarkation for England. See dispatch no. 334, dated London, January 4, 1814, AHN/E, legajo 5466. In his dispatch, he enclosed a note from one of the Spaniards marooned at Brielle, Corporal Manuel Amor, requesting assistance from the Spanish minister: "The unhappy situation in which all of these men find themselves, almost nude, without money with which to support their most basic needs, sleeping on the ground without a bed or any cover whatsoever, and the vivid desire that we all have to leave this land and return to Spain so that we can once again bear arms and take our revenge on the oppressor of our august sovereign . . . oblige me now to take the liberty of addressing myself to Your Excellency." They would soon be sent to Plymouth and from there to San Sebastián in Spain. See dispatch no. 348, dated London, January 25, 1814, AHN/E, legajo 5466; and copy of letter from Major General Brown to the Commander of the Western District, Citadel, Plymouth, January 23, 1814, British National Archives, WO 1/658.

the yoke of the French, was assaulted by the populace and completely plundered. No windows nor doors remained in it for what had escaped the hands of the Dutch could not escape the more destructive ones of the Spaniards. Nothing but dirt or filth could be seen there.

Among my old acquaintances I met there Mr. Bausa, Mr. Hernández, Mr. Rubio, Mr. Castañeda and many others. Rubio and those who lived in his room were the strongest party in the house, and they were proud to admit us to their club as we were gentlemen and respectively rich. We chose a room in which our soldiers put the beds given to us by the Commandant, which by the by I was long ago acquainted with. They were exactly like those we had in the barracks of prisoners in France, for both were the same used by the French soldiers. Then for our meals we did as our friends: we gave our rations to a poor woman of the neighbourhood who for a few half pence dressed them, and furnished plate, napkins, etc. This day our dinner was rather late for we could not get the rations at the usual hour of the morning, having arrived after it. But as wine, gin and bread was plentiful in our friends' room we wanted nothing, besides the conversation was so interesting that we could have forgotten our hunger. The reader of this sketch must know that every one of our friends had as long a story and perhaps more interesting to tell: then we had a great subject of conversation in the abuse of those of our countrymen who had been in the French service and now were there endeavouring to go with us, tho' we wanted to prevent them. Another subject of conversation was to try and discipline a little the soldiers we had there for nothing could be more wild and savage than them. And the most interesting of all subjects was that of our embarkment.

The first and only transport had sailed a few days ago and there was no hope of having another soon, for the Commandant had no power about it, the English Captain said he had none to dispose of, and the Court of Hague to which Spaniards sent an Embassy had not answered yet. The current opinion was that as there was an English Packet sailing twice a week from Hellevoetsluis, it was their interest not to give us a transport that those who could afford it should pay for this passage. This scheme was too mean to be devised and carried on by the English nation so I thought it nonsense, yet it might very well be managed by the secondary Agents, for it produced more than twice the money which they usually got, for the packet was always crowded.

In spite of all we heard we resolved to go to Hellevoetsluis and speak to Captain King. Mr. Manuel and I were appointed for this commission, which we undertook next morning of our arrival. We walked to Hellevoetsluis by a pleasant road of bricks as I have already described and in about two hours we were at the gates of this little town. The guard asked our papers and we gave them the first we had at hand—the note of the Consul for Capt. King. It was sufficient. The entrance of the town is slightly fortified: the harbour is within it, for it is nothing else but a broad and deep canal with sluices to keep the water during the low water. Over this canal there is a Drawbridge the first I have seen of its kind for instead of being lifted, its two halves roll horizontally to both sides and leave a free passage to the ships. After we had breakfasted we called on Capt. King. He is very tall this man with an air of carelessness quite striking to eyes accustomed to the French *empressement* [alacrity]. He looks at the Consul's paper and said he had no transports nor knew when he could get them, but as in this moment the Packet Agent entered the room he said to us that that gentleman could provide for our passage. I asked if it was for the account of government, to which he answered it would be for our own account. I thanked him for the advice and took leave of them, not before they had paid me a compliment upon my good English; how sincerely anybody may judge.

With these bad tidings we came back to our companions whom we found very busy about one of the bad Spaniards who wanted to live among us. He was notified to quit immediately before we came to ruder means. Another thing about which they were also busy was the organization of our soldiers who became quarrelsome and even riotous. This was not to be wondered if we consider that the Spanish soldiers naturally wild become more so by the ill usage they experience in France. Here they had been taught to submit not to what was right but to force, and as now they saw no force they would not obey. They had also lost the respect for their officers from having seen them in the state of dejection of prisoners: to which we must add as another cause of insubordination their having served many in the French army.

Our club resolved to ask of the Commandant the superintendance of them, which was solicited next day and granted, but rather late for already in that night a sergeant had been stabbed by a soldier. Our first act of authority was to put him in prison, but he was impudent enough to laugh all the way to prison at the officer who took him there and menace him he would murder him as soon as he could find an opportunity. This day (18th March) was employed in looking at the fortification of the town and in resolving whether we were to go by the packet or not. The discussion was long for tho' we had money enough to pay it, this expense would take more than half of our stock, which might be wanting for some ulterior occurrences. At last the fear of remaining long in so bad company and that of going topsy-turvy in a transport with all kind of people prevailed against our economy and resolved to go next day (the 19th) to secure our places in the Packet. I must not forget a laughable occurrence which I met with during my stay at Brielle: as my beard was too long and I had no means of shaving myself I went to a shaving shop. I saw but women in it, so I expected to see the barber coming. Not at all, the old woman undertook the task and did it so ill that I could not bear it. I complained but she continued to flay me without shaving me.

The 19th, as I was saying, we went to Hellevoetsluis to secure our places. Before this our passport was to be revised by the Commissary and Capt. King. The first gave immediately his signature but Capt. King, who was rather tipsy could not know what for was his signature wanted, yet as we assured him it was so he wrote, or rather scribbled, "there can be no objection in permitting the bearers to go to England in the Packet." The cause of his being tipsy must be that as the Duchess of Oldenburg had arrived there as also the Duke of Clarence with a frigate to take her to England, he might perhaps have been of the grand dinner, in which surely the good wine was not wanting [lacking]. With these two signatures we were admitted to pay £ 2.14.6 each for our place. My heart was broken to see my poor money in the hands of that merciless Englishman. We went to the Packet to secure our beds. The Capt. said we had only three, but he would make *comfortable* the other. I will not forget his comforts. We left that place to go to Brielle and tell our companions that all was ready to put to sail next day in the morning. The other gentlemen looked at us with envy and more so our poor Estevan, whom we could not take with us for the great expense not only of the passage but of the rest of our journey, where we did not want him, not having a carriage. However, we told him to come with us next day to the Port and if there was a lower price for servants we would take him with us. At all events we gave him a guinea and a sword to repay him for his good services, telling him that we would give him more if we could.

I could scarcely sleep with the fear that the Packet would sail without us: so early in the morning I was hurrying to my companions to go to Hellevoetsluis. Some of our friends came with us to see us go, but they did not obtain it, for the wind not being fair and the fog being too thick we were deluded during all the morning by the Captain with the hopes of putting to sail until at last by noon he said we could not sail until next day. Our friends then and poor Estevan took leave of us, and we remained to wander about in the town. As we had had a late and copious breakfast we did not think of our dinner until three or four o'clock, hour at which all ordinaries in the town were over. The first place to which we applied for dinner was the house in which we had breakfasted three times. There we were answered pretty civilly they could not give us a dinner. After this we applied to every coffee house, and every inn in the town and could not find nor dinner nor a polite answer. My rage was unutterable when I saw this cursed country in which I must starve having money in my pocket. When all our hopes were lost we met a poor man who had showed me the day before an alehouse, and applied to him now for knowing where we could get a dinner. He took us to the same

Alehouse where the good woman said she could not cook anything else but beefstakes and potatoes. Beefstakes! said I to me, what can she give us better? Come, come, let us have beefstakes. We made a comfortable dinner of them and paid not much.

For the sake of economy as well as for the fear of being refused beds in the inns, or of missing the packet next day, I contrived to go and sleep in the packet. We applied to the Captain who made some objections thinking we wanted to be fed too, but when he knew we wanted it not he admitted us on board. He was drinking tea with his son, a fine lad. We were offered to drink it with them but did not accept of it. When they had done, they went on shore, and we went to bed. They were not very comfortable, tho' they seemed to me too good for onboard a ship. I shuddered with cold during all the night and longed to see the day to get up. I went upon deck and had the good news of the wind being fair and the fog being away.

Now the passengers began to arrive and each other's curiosity to be excited. Each began to display his own character, and the cold observer had a good employment. I could be called cold observer because I was observing and shuddering with cold at the same time. The packet became so crowded that we could scarcely move within it. It may be easily conceived by saying that there was room only for 18 persons and we were more than 40. We had among the passengers some English gentlemen and officers, many German fugitives from Hamburg, a few Dutch and Italian, and many Spaniards, together with other people whom I took no notice of. Of the English officers a young one interested me much. He was going back home because as he was coming to Holland in the beginning of the winter his feet were frozen and after two months confinement, seeing he could not recover he obtained permission to come to England. He went to bed as soon as he came on board and did not stir from it until we landed.

An old Major attracted my attention by a trait of what we consider in the continent the true English character. He was leaning his back on the bordo [*sic*] of the ship, and speaking with the English gentlemen when a rope passing near him throwed overboard his traveling cap.

Everybody was moved by this inevitable loss, but the Major did not even look. He continued his conversation with the same indifference, without thinking of putting on anything until the servant of one of the English gentlemen brought to him a cap of his master.

The Italian or soi-disant German was the buffoon of the party. He dressed and undressed many times only to show his clothes, sang, plaid the flute and did everything to attract the notice. His flute was the first of Monzani's I have seen. He played very well, which, together with the great number of keys, the ignorant audience admired. Yet Mr. Peter who was conscious that I was a match to him teased me to take out my flute and challenge him. At last after breakfast when we were in the main sea sailing nine miles, when all the people were under deck I yielded and proposed the Italian to play a duet. Now the admiration turned on my side for people wondered that a ragged fellow with a plain flute could do as much, or more than the fine fellow, since I plaid his music. This made me enter into conversation with the highest character on board, Mr. [blank] Marquis of [blank] and Mariscal de Campo of the Spanish army. He is of an Italian family therefore he had a fondness for music and for the Italian language and as he thought I excelled in both he conceived a high opinion of me. I supported it by some happy observations I had the good luck to make upon the subject of two *bad Spaniards* who had stealed within the packet; and by treating him with the respect due to his rank for it has been always my maxim not to permit my inferior [blank][61] but in the same time not be wanting in the regards due to my superior. In general while my head has had the command I have always respected property. But let us not anticipate in the methodical account of my voyage.

We sailed at about nine in the morning of the 21st of March, with fair wind tho' little. Everything seemed to combine to give me a grand show of the sea for the first time. The little fog we had in leaving the shore was like a curtain to veil us the scene and show it all at once for when we were out of sight of land the fog disappeared, the sun shone,

61. Written above blank: "*me manquer.*"

A Dutch Packet in a Rising Breeze, by Thomas Rowlandson (1756–1827). This is the transport that Fernando used to get over to England. (Yale Center for British Art, Paul Mellon Collection)

the wind blew fairer, and the sea had no more agitation than what is wanted to give it life. I was struck with the grandeur of the spectacle for more than an hour in which I never felt satisfied of looking at the immensity, which surrounded me. Secondary objects added some interest to this scene as were the black big fishes swimming and jumping all along with us, and some poor sparrows taking hospitality in our sails. The English gentleman put some bread and water on the boat that they might eat it without being frightened. I then heard for the first time that tender manner in the English language of calling *things* to animate beings. I never have forgotten it and have made use of it in my most fond moments. It conveys a great meaning to my heart. For instance, I could not say a more fond expression to a woman than *sweet little thing for love.* I leave English ears to judge of the exactness of the expression but as for my meaning if I was to make a language of my own I could not express it better than with this words as I feel them.

I got acquainted with a very genteel person who spoke so good Spanish as to be mistaken for a Spaniard. He was French but had been for many years established at Madrid, and only left it when the French army was driven from Spain. His politeness captivated me. He wanted us to partake of his provisions but dinner was preparing and I refused him. What I would have accepted was some wine for in the Packet there was none to be had for any money, not even beer. I cannot bear water therefore I was during 24 hours without any beverage but tea. It was rather tantalizing to see the English gentlemen who went upon deck after dinner and drank till night. The Italian partook of their bottles but not for nothing for he served for their amusement. They made him enter in philosophical disputes to puzzle him until he was in a passion and then laughed at him. About dark they asked us to play but I would not accompany a man who was the amusement of the company, excusing myself with sickness. I really felt so and had felt it now and then during the day but never completely. The tea cured me this time. Many people by this time were quite sick, among others a pretty young girl who was the maid of the late sister of the Marshal and now was his mistress. She was upon deck while her master and lover was below. Every young man came to cajole her, Mr. Peter among them with such impudence that she was obliged to go under deck. Mr. Peter continued his suit even after we landed: the old lover was extremely jealous, and wanted to get rid of him at any rate. This was the reason why Mr. Peter remained so long at Harwich, for the Marshal did not send to the Ambassador Mr. Peter's petition that he might remain behind.

We had on board some other women, one of them very interesting: she was the wife of a merchant Captain who had been a prisoner for many years in France. There they had got all their children. They had escaped when the armies entered France and were upon their return home.

The wind began to blow less and less in the night until it began to change. I went up and down to inquire but could have no intelligence. The Captain prisoner appeared very uneasy about the weather. I daresay only because he was too anxious to get home, for the weather continued very fair. Now everybody who had a bed had gone to it, but those who had not, and these were the greatest number, came to the cabins and crowded them in such a manner that there was scarcely room to sit, but when we began to feel sleepy and wanted to lay on the floor we found the impossibility of stretching one's self. To this inconvenience we must add the noise of those who spent the night playing whist: in short there was no possibility of sleeping even for those as myself who were in great want of it. I longed to see the day in hopes that people would leave the cabin and of descrying the English shore.

The day began to appear and a high wind and boisterous sea with it such as to overturn chairs and tables within the cabin, and as I felt very sick I went up to the open air. I then saw very near for the first time the longed-for English shore, which I hailed with all my heart, not for its interesting appearance, for nothing can be less pleasing to the sight than it, but because I saw in it a shelter to my liberty and the first place after so many years where I could give way to the feelings inspired by the ties of nature.

We had deviated in our course a few miles to the north of Harwich. So now we were obliged to sail along the coast towards Harwich. A Convoy was sailing towards the north offering a very pretty prospect. We were gradually less and less tost about until we noticed we were in the Harbour. Harwich was seen on the left with no other charms than those that any town offers to those who have been at sea. Its appearance was not new to me for it looked to me as for the buildings, quite like Gibraltar. The water is too shallow for ships to approach the wharfs so we waited for boats to take us on shore. One came and took all the luggage, to my great astonishment, until I knew that nobody was the master of taking with himself anything before it went to the custom house. This was for me new and shocking for in Spain they are not at all particular about wearing apparel, or anything for private use. I parted with my little bag containing all my property. Every passenger was landed before ourselves, for as soon as we intended to get into a boat, the boatsman said to us, "no, no, we'll take the Spaniards all together." I thought this was because we were not to pay but I saw it was only because they wanted to give the preference to their countrymen for we paid as much as anybody.

The hardships of the passage together with these marks of the English marks [*sic*] of the English pride put me in a bad mood, such as not to enjoy the pleasure of landing but by reflection. This bad mood increased at every step I took in the place for everything was against me. We learnt that in England the military men were not lodged in private houses and that there was nothing provided for us. The Spanish Consul told us all this, showing us at the same time a letter of our Ambassador saying that his friend Garcia[s] could not make any more supplies for the expenses incurred by the Spaniards in England.[62] What shall we then do, said we? Shall we die? "You shall be in the barracks," said the Consul. As he was speaking French and improperly used the word *barraque* [*sic*] instead of *caserne* we were shocked at the mere proposal.[63] *"Quoi, dans des barraques, Monsieur?"* said I; *"les français nous traiteront mieux que vous qui vous vantez d'etre nos alliés. Des barraques!!"* ["What, in the barracks, Monsieur?" . . . "The French

62. Juan Garcias, the commissioner in charge of the local treasury, dispensed money to the first Spanish deserters and escapees to arrive in the English ports, beginning at the end of 1813. For example, the Spanish minister Fernán-Núñez reported that Garcias helped ninety-three Spanish deserters from the French army, who came by way of Coburg, as well as eleven men and officers escaped from the depots. In cooperation with the British government, the Spanish officials acted to have their countrymen returned to Spain as quickly as possible from Plymouth to the Spanish port city of San Sebastián. See dispatch no. 333, dated London, January 4, 1814, AHN/E 5466. The Spanish government did authorize extraordinary funds requested by Fernán-Núñez but not until mid-February 1814 (see introduction). Based on Fernando and the Porres brothers' reception, it seems that the monies had not reached London or the port cities where the Spaniards were arriving. Indeed, on January 25, Fernán-Núñez reported that Garcias would no longer dispense money until he received funds from the Spanish government. AHN/E, legajo 5466, dispatch 348. Well into June of that year, Fernán-Núñez and Garcias requested funds and, when told that they had been dispatched, reported that none had arrived.

63. A *barraque* was a flimsy, temporary structure, while a *caserne* was a permanent military barrack.

treated us better than you, who claim to be our allies. Barracks!!"] exclaimed all at once. The Consul had not a word to answer but to send us to the military Commandant. Our Marshal and some others were admitted to him. I do not know what passed between them only I saw an aide-de-camp who took us all about the town I do not know for what purpose, speaking of us to all his acquaintance who met him, with high contempt, as he thought none of us could understand him.

I was fired with this abuse and therefore remained behind cursing him and England altogether. I do not remember well if he took us again to the Consul or if we went by ourselves. I only remember that we obtained at last that he would stand answerable for us or rather for our government in an inn for our board and lodging. He came with us and made us promise before the innkeeper that we would not exact more than the ordinary at the rate of 7/6 per day. This manner of dealing was too mean not to mortify me as well as to see the innkeeper taking off the carpet of the parlour, which he destined us. Then the news that we could not come to London without a particular permission of the Ambassador, which he very seldom granted, was enough by itself to give an aversion for England. We made our petition to the Ambassador, stating that we would come at our own expense and trusted it to the Marshal.

After all this was done we sat to breakfast in a very ill humour, which all of a sudden was changed into a delicious rapture by a letter of my brother, brought to me by the Consul, in which he said to me I wanted no passport being a *British subject* and that I might take the money I wanted for my journey to London. In vain I would attempt to describe those rapturous moments. I became talkative and forward as is always the case with me in great joys. Everything smiled to me, even the haughty Britons who half an hour before looked at me with contempt showed now all sort of regards. The innkeeper went with me all about the town for my business, and I shall never forget the satisfaction with which he said to Capt. McDonough of the Diana Packet, in which was come, "don't you know that he (pointing to me) is an Englishman!" "Indeed!!" answered the Capt. "Well I am happy to know it," added he and shook me very cordially by the hand. My head was so giddy that I cannot keep an exact recollection of the numberless events of that day. I was obliged to make an affidavit, to go to the customhouse to give our passports and answer to a great many questions, to go to take some money, and God knows how many others. I had like to have lost the fruit of all my exertions for being too late with the affidavit to the Director of the Alien Office. The office was shut: I then called upon him at his house but not knowing the manners of the Country I gave a single knock and my reception was according to my knock. The servant would not let me in, but my entreaties were so pressing that the Gentleman came to the door and as I was already an Englishman recommended by Gordon Murphy and Co. he took me to the drawing room.[64] His wife was there. I looked at her and my eyes were dazzled, yet this was a feeble impression compared with what I have afterwards experienced in London.

I obtained permission to come to London for which I began immediately to prepare: then I went to dinner during which a very comical scene took place. The two *bad Spaniards* who came with us in the Packet had followed us step by step in all we had done at Harwich that they might enjoy the same privileges with the good Spaniards, but the Marshal had told them that they should forbear their company at our dinner, because people of so different opinions could not agree well. The innkeeper did not choose to give separate dinners so he put their *couverts* in our table. When we saw them we took them off and sat by ourselves. At that instant we saw the oldest of the two coming to us sobbing and faltering that he wanted the Chaplain who was in

64. Col. Juan Murphy, like Fernando and Joseph, was a Spaniard of Irish origin. His firm took a leading role in trade with Mexico. Fernando worked in the firm until his return to Seville two years later. On Gordon and Murphy, see Martin Murphy, "The Murphys of Waterford, Malaga, Mexico and London," *Irish Genealogist* 13, no. 3 (2012): 210–11. Juan Murphy also helped the Porres brothers secure their return to Spain via Plymouth. See Fernando's note to Murphy dated March 29, 1814, in Blanco White Family Collection, Princeton.

our company to confess him for he had very few minutes of life. He said it so earnestly that I suspected him to have taken some poison out of despair. The Chaplain would not go because he was afraid of him, thinking he wanted only to assassinate him and there arose the most laughable dispute between the dying man and the Priest. We prevailed upon him to go and see what that man wanted. They went out for a moment and got rid of him. It was not so with his companion, for he came bragging and telling bravadoes, to which, conscious of our superiority, we answered with a cold contempt, yet as the innkeeper would not give him a separate dinner we let him sit with us.

Just after dinner the Landlord came to hurry me for going to the Coach. I ran to it without taking leave of anybody but the Porres followed me to tell me farewell, and I really felt uncomfortable in parting with so good friends with whom I had lived so long, but it consoled me to think that I had left them all my money, that of my Mother excepted. The coach in which I was coming was not the public stage but an extraordinary one sent upon a particular circumstance, and so much so that there were six horses to it, which I have never seen afterwards in England. The only person in it was a tall, fat Dutchman, who had come in the Packet with me and against whom I had an aversion because he was telling false stories about the monks in Spain; besides, he was an ill-tempered man so that I had no reason to be pleased with his company, yet it proved most advantageous to me and agreeable for as he knew the language and manners of the country he could extricate me from the scrap in which we were. In the course of our conversation we discovered we were connected long ago. Not only he knew Seville and my house, but Mr. Purden, a young Englishman who had been learning in my father's counting house had been afterwards his Partner.

We started from Harwich at 5 o'clock in the evening of the 22nd March in a great speed but before we had come to the first stage it was night and so dark that the coachman drove the coach into a deep ditch and was half overturned. It gave time to get out without the least injury but the difficulty laid in taking off the coach from the mud. We tried every means without success, while our Dutchman was cursing and swearing incessantly, and reproaching the men for not having put lanterns to the coach as he had told them. I was vexed with this delay and little hope I had of seeing an end to this. At last they brought fresh horses and put them to the back of the coach, then beat them most unmercifully. These powerful horses made an effort and snatched away the Coach from the mud. The spectators made resound the air with a cry of applause, but the joy was short, for the horses bewildered with the strokes ran away with the coach, overturned it and broke it to pieces. Here began my real anxiety for I knew not what was to become of us. "'Tis no matter," said the Dutchman, when he saw the impossibility of getting on with that coach, "we'll have a portchaise at the expense of the owner of the Stage, for I have been promised to be tomorrow at 8 o'clock in London."

As the accident had happened near a village we entered a poor inn until they got for us a portchaise. My companion asked for us some cheese and Porter, which he found delicious. I would have found them so, if I had not been rather indisposed of the sea, for I remember the porter was good. The portchaise came and we drove to a large town whose name I do not recollect. The Postillion took us into a grand inn, almost like a town, waiters better dressed than ourselves came to us, but when they saw we wanted nothing they went to bed and left us in a parlour. The owner of the coach lived in that town and we sent him a message to have another. He said he could but it was long before he came. The Dutchman rang the bell a hundred times and scolded the servants but nothing could be obtained until about two o'clock in the morning. We started at this hour having in our company the fat owner of our coach. With the approaching day I began to see the aspect of the English country, which in winter is not very favourable. We stopped at an inn for breakfast and there my companion made a bother because they wanted to give us some ham besides the coffee we have asked, which made me laugh for the oddity of his character, wishing always to scold. I made myself here as clean as possible to make a fair appearance in London, and pursued our journey with fine weather.

We drove at a great rate in order to fulfill as much as possible the engagement but it was not before twelve o'clock of the 23rd March 1814 I descried London. I was within it without being aware of it, for after we had gone through a village (such seemed to me) for more than a mile I asked the owner of the Coach, "how do you call this village?" to which he very coldly replied, "London." The mere name of London flurried me. I felt as I think must feel a young maid at the approach of the moment in which she is going to lose forever that name. Never I had thought myself more distant from my brother nor deemed so difficult to see him, yet I dreaded the first sight of him, our first word more than death. I would have given the whole world that this first terrible moment had been past, or rather that there would not be a first moment in such a meeting. I longed for the second moment and hated the first.

In this anxiety I teased my companion and the coachman about the Edgware Road, and about Hackney Coaches, for my brother had written to me to take one of them when I was in London. My Dutchman, who owing to the connections we had discovered between us had shown some affection for me, told me to be quiet that he would do everything for me until he had put me into a Hackney coach. When we entered the most frequented streets, I began to lose patience with the frequent stops of the Stage, until there was such a stoppage that the Dutchman thought better to get out and walk along Cheapside. I was in the oddest garb for English eyes as I noticed in the staring of the country people as we were coming, and by the frequent observations of my Dutchman, who used to say, not knowing the exact force of the words, "*vous seriez bel homme si vous afiez [sic] vous moustaches* (You would be *tall* [*sic*] if you cut off your moustaches)," notwithstanding nobody looked at me in Cheapside. I coveted every hackney coach and thought every one the last I was to find, therefore I teased my companion to get me one. He yielded to my prayers, called one, told me a very cordial farewell, and gave the coachman the direction. Now by myself in a coach, most shockingly jolted all along this immense town I felt myself as if I was left in a bark in the immensity of a boisterous sea, without hopes of ever discovering the longed for shore. I looked all the names of the streets and saw nothing but Oxford St. for an age. I was seeing the end of the town and no appearance of the only spot I wanted. At last I see the name of Edgware Road but the numbers increased slowly. The 67 comes, the door is open, I am in the drawing room but my brother is not there. A few minutes of anguish passed before he entered the room. "Pepe!" faintly uttered I, "Hermano mio!" said he and we sprang in each other's arms.

Oh! you most tender of beings for whom I have undertaken this laborious task, oh fancy the delicious moments which ensued; fancy them for they could not be uttered: and when your imagination have decked them with the most powerful charms, then I will pray Heaven to bless you every day with still sweeter raptures.

Tabernacle Row 21st February 1815.

INDEX

Note: Page numbers in *italics* refer to illustrations; those followed by "n" indicate diary footnotes or endnotes to the introduction.